Power Points
for
Increase

BOB HARRISON

Editor's Note: Many of the news stories and features that appear in power Points for Increase have been abridged. They have been edited and/or paraphrased for the sake of brevity and clarity.

Unless otherwise indicated, all Scripture quotations are taken from the King James Version of the Bible. Scripture quotations marked (NKJV) are taken from the *New King James Version*, © 1979, 1980, 1982 by Thomas Nelson Inc. Used by permission. All rights reserved. Scripture quotations marked (NIV) are from the Holy Bible, *New International Version*, © 1973, 1978, 1984 by the International Bible Society. Used by permission. Scripture quotations marked (NASB) are from the *New American Standard Bible*®· © 1960, 1962, 1963, 1968, 1971, 1972, 1973, 1975, 1977, 1988 by Lockman Foundation. Used by permission. (www.Lockman. org). Scripture quotations marked (TLB) are taken from The Living Bible, © 1971. Used by permission of Tyndale House Publishers, Inc., Wheaton, Illinois 60189. All rights reserved.

POWER POINTS FOR INCREASE

ISBN-13: 978-1-60683-018-5

ISBN-10: 1-60683-018-X

© 2010 by Bob Harrison

Harrison International Seminars

2109 East 69th Street, Tulsa, OK 74136

1-800-632-4653 • 918-496-3399

e-mail: Increase@increase.org

website: www.increase.org

15 14 13 12 11 10   10 9 8 7 6 5 4 3 2 1

Published by Harrison House Publishers

P.O. Box 35035

Tulsa, OK 74153

www.harrisonhouse.com

Acknowledgments

Over one million copies of my best-selling teaching audio programs on "increase thinking" have been sold. I am very appreciative of my friends and peers who challenged me to increase the influence of my life by adding books such as this to my arsenal of teaching.

A heartfelt thanks goes to some of my fellow speakers and mentors who continue to have such an influence on my life including: Zig Ziglar—The Greatest Motivational Speaker I have ever shared the stage with; Peter Lowe—America's Premier Success Seminar Conductor, who constantly challenges me to stretch my influence; Brian Klemmer—Superachiever Geru for his continuing encouragement and valuable insights; Joe Ninowski—for introducing me to "The Book" that has most changed and impacted my life; plus John Bevere and Myles Munroe whose repeated sharing at my Increase Events have such a great positive influence on me and achievers from across the globe. In addition I want to thank other major career influencers on my life such as Mark Victor Hansen, Dexter Yeager, Billy Graham, Tom Hopkins, Norman Schwarzkopf, Robert Schuller, Ralph Wilkerson, Ed Gungor, Bernie Dohrmann, and John Mason.

Also, I want to share my appreciation to the Premier Members of my "Increase Team" from around the world whose changed lives and financial support have encouraged and motivated me more than they will ever know.

In addition, a special thanks goes to my executive assistants Jodi Cook-Bailey and Kari Bloom who assisted me so much with research and author communications.

I also want to acknowledge my father and mother, Dr. Irvine and Edna Harrison, who are now deceased, but who provided me with a loving, stable home, and a spiritual foundation that continues to positively impact me every day of my life.

A double portion of gratitude goes to my five children, their four spouses, plus my deceased wife, Cindy, for their continual encouragement and inspiration. And of course my wife, Sharon, whose love brightens my days and whose commitment to excellence stirs me to increase even more.

Working with Harrison House has been an author's dream. Thanks to Troy Wormell for all his input and enthusiasm for this project. Twenty-five years ago Troy was my road manager. Now he is a mega-printing company owner, publisher and successful investor. Also, thanks to my son-in-law Chris Ophus, Director of Marketing, who has spent countless hours advising me on marketing strategies over the years and for his work on this project .

Lastly, here I want to express my gratitude to you. If you, and others like you who desire to improve your lives, did not purchase this book, all my hours of research and writing would be "in vain." I pray that the strategies revealed in this book will positively impact you as they have so many others.

Contents

Preface... 13

Power Point 1: Massive Chrysler Shutdown................................. 18
    Bob Harrison   Fresh Source of Supply

Power Point 2: Wrong House Raided.. 20
    Colin Powell   Flexibility and Decision Making

Power Point 3: Plane Loses Door in Flight.................................... 22
    Dick Withnell   Controlling Interruptions

Power Point 4: Nails Removed From Man's Head 24

    John Maxwell   Negative Attitude Prevention Keys

Power Point 5: Giuliani Starts Investment Firm............................. 26
    Rudolph Giuliani   Starting Small with Success

Power Point 6: Last Pontiac Rolls Off Line.................................. 28

    General Norman Schwarzkopf   "A collection of seasons"

Power Point 7: Teen Surfs After Shark Attack 30

    Bethany Hamilton   Overcoming Adversity

Power Point 8: Zig Ziglar Receives Award 32

    Zig Ziglar   Personal Increase Strategies

Power Point 9: Government's Eye Never Sleeps 34

    T.D. Jakes   The Dangers of Faitgue

Power Point 10: Charity Gets Moving in New Van 36
    Anthony Robbins   Persevering Through Negatives

Power Point 11: Survival Attitude Helps Downed Pilot................. 38

    Dexter Yager   Developing a Survival Attitude

Power Points 12: England's Bobbies May Discard Helmets........... 40

    Lady Margaret Thatcher   The Defensive Mind-Set

Power Points 13: Resort Town Bans Ties...................................... 42

    Mary Lou Retton   Being Ready for Opportunity

Power Points 14: Collision with Pole Restores Eyesight 44

    Jerome Edmondson   Activating Your Dreams

Power Points 15: Swimmers Told Not to Spit in Pool 46

    Tamara Lowe   Weathering Life's Storms

Power Point 16: Man Searches for Absentee Dad 48

    Lee Iacocca   Absentee Dads

Power Point 17: Doctors Warned About Exploding Patients 50

    Bob Harrison   Defeating Anger

Power Point 18: Turtle Falls From Sky 52

    Ruth Stafford Peale   Keeping Your Grip

Power Point 19: Swimmer Loses Trunks During Race 54

    David Mayo   Responding to Negative Events

Power Point 20: Fish Removed From Man's Nose 56

    Les Brown   Creating Hunger to Succeed

Power Point 21: Cadillac Crashes Into Bedroom 58

    Dr. Joyce Brothers   The Power of Knowledge

Power Point 22: Governor Schwarzennggar Announces Plan 60

    Bob Harrison   Achieving Goals Strategies

Power Point 23: Blind Man Robs Bank, Then Cannot Find Way Out 62

    Bob Harrison   Having an Exit Strategy

Power Point 24: Stocks Ignoring Bad Economic News 64

    Bill Swad   Your Decision to Succeed

Power Point 25: Joe Gibbs Rejoins NASCAR 66

    Robert Townsend   Making Right Things Happen

Power Point 26: 92 Year Old Woman Gets 30-Year Mortgage 68

    John Mason   The Future-Focused Mindset

Power Point 27: Man Hit by Lightening on Golf Course 70

    Rich DeVos   The Gift of Encouragement

Power Point 28: Man Comes Out of Coma 72

    Rock Harrison   Self-Image and Performance

Power Point 29: Toilet Paper Theft Causes Firing 74

    Jess Gibson   Developing Character

Power Point 30: Car Falls Seven Floors..76

    Dr. Robert Schuller   A Positive Approach to Living

Power Point 31: Couple Marries at Airport..78

    Lynette Lewis   Be Ready for the Unexpected

Power Point 32: Government Cares for Monkeys...80

    Dr. Kenneth Blanchard   Avoiding Unnecessary Tasks

Power Point 33: Man Watches TV for Five Years...82

    Dr. Robert Rutherford   Understanding Mortgage Time

Power Point 34: Quarterback Leaves Pro Bowl Early 84

    Sandy Harrison-Redmond   The Art of Reframing

Power Point 35: With Low-cal Movement, Less is More 86

    Robert Crandall   Pruning for Greater Output

Power Point 36: Palm Desert Buys University..88

    Brian Klemmer   Intention+ Mechanism = Results

Power Point 37: Bugging Devices Cause Political Furor...............................90

    Bob Harrison   Safeguarding Important Information

Power Point 38: Parents Made Kids Eat Rats and Roaches 92

    Bob Harrison   Words and Self-image

Power Point 39: New Lease on Life..94

    Edna Harrison-Harlin   Rebounding From Grief

Power Point 40: Man Hugs Tree to Escape Fine...96

    Dewey Friedel   Hugs and Positive Touches

Power Point 41: Amateur Golfer Shoots 59 98

    Peter Lowe   Success Strategies

Power Point 42: Survivors Gather at Reunion 100

    Capt. 'Sully' Sullenberger   Responding to Crisis

Power Point 43: Giant Sinkhole Swallows Home..102

    Bob Harrison   Relationship Reinforcement Strategies

Power Point 44: Biggest Loser Wins Big 104
Gary Richardson   Willingness to Pay the Price

Power Point 45: New York Cabbie's Check Bounces 106
 Bob Harrison   Loss-Prevention Tactics

Power Point 46: Cruise Ship Runs Aground 108
 Gavin and Patty MacLeod Marriage Enrichment Game Plan

Power Point 47: City Starts Automated Trash Removal 110
 Bob Harrison   Paper Reduction Systems

Power Point 48: Graham Awarded Congressional Medal 112
 Billy Graham   Character and Reputation

Power Point 49: Asian Elephant Born in Captivity 114
 Myles Monroe   Investing in Your Future

Power Point 50: Woman Rides Out Tornado in Bathtub 116
 Sue Boss   Overcoming Adversity

Power Point 51: Airline Sends Kids to Wrong Cities 118
 Steven Covey   End in Mind Planning

Power Point 52: Cities Finding Gold in Parking Fees and Fines 120
 Bob Harrison   Product-Added Increase

Power Point 53: Governor Says "Thanks" to Firms 122
 Bob Harrison   Showing Appreciation

Power Point 54: Man Gets Free Trip to Hawaii 124
 Tim Storey   Where to Find the Big Things

Power Point 55: Women Trapped in Elevator for Three Days 126
 Aaron Lewis   The Answer is Within You

Power Point 56: Dallas Cowboys Coach Was Pure Class 128
 Tom Landry   Creating a Winning Team

Power Point 57: Can Found Inside of Fish 130
 Bob Harrison   Knowing That You Can

Power Point 58: Postal Truck Plunges Into Pool 132
 Bob Harrison   Protecting Against Theft

Power Point 59: Student Jailed for Udder Nonsense.................................... 134

    Eastman Curtis   Creating "Motion"

Power Point 60: Plane That Crashed Was on Autopilot 136

    Ed Gungor   Is it Our Work or God's Sovereignty?

Power Point 61: Vegetarians Becoming Flexitarians 138

    Bob Harrison   Protecting Against Theft

Power Point 62: Doorman Refuses to Hail Cab 140

    Dr. Kenneth Cooper   The Benefits of Exercise

Power Point 63: Woman Living in Man's Closet 142

    Bob Harrison   Advantages of Delegation

Power Point 64: Dead Woman Gets Job Back 144

    Arvella Schuller   Keeping On Track

Power Point 65: Saboteurs Derail Train 146

    Steven Covey   Eliminating Time Wasters

Power Point 66: Ancient Jewelry Found Near Dead Sea 148

    Edwin Louis Cole   Creating Good out of Bad Situations

Power Point 67: Globe Littered With Land Mines 150

    Bob Harrison   Overcoming Negative Words and Opinions

Power Point 68: Contest Officials Search for God 152

    Florence Littaeur   Appreciating People's Differences

Power Point 69: Varmints Stink Up School 154

    Dr. Phil McGraw   Dealing With Foul Friends

Power Points 70: Chic-fil-A Wins Quality Award 156

    S. Truett Cathy   It's Easier to Succeed Than Fail

Power Point 71: $2 Million Paid for Lunch 158

    Bob Harrison   Maximizing Encounters with Celebrities

Power Point 72: Many Still in The Dark 160

    James Stovall   Gaining Greater Vision

Power Point 73: Elevator Suddenly Plunges 162

    Ken Kerr   The Value of Repeat Sales

Power Point 74: Star is Rich and Lonely......164

    Catherine Marshall   Defeating Lonliness

Power Point 75: Star Has Deathbed Regrets......166

    Dr. Irvine Harrison   Leaving a Good Heritage?

Power Point 76: Student Honesty Linked to Discounts......168

    George Reece   The Value of Integrity

Power Point 77: Sheriff is Resident of Jail He Built......170

    Tim Flynn   Unlocking Limiting Beliefs

Power Point 78: Bush Parachutes for His 80th Birthday......172

    George H.W. Bush   Improving Marriage Relationships

Power Point 79: Arab Sheik Buys 40 College Degrees......174

    Wendy Murakami   The Rewards of Innovation

Power Point 80: Jet Crashes Short of Runway......176

    Bob Harrison   Avoiding Burnout

Power Point 81: Wife Victimized by Chiseling Romeo......178

    James Guinn   Don't Be the Next Victim

Power Point 82: Bird Causes Power Outage at Airport......180

    Dennis Byrd   Winning Against Adversity

Power Point 83: Man Trapped in Outhouse Overnight......182

    George Shinn   Eliminating Time Wasters

Power Point 84: Smart Money Does Not Jingle......184

    Bob Harrison   Increasing Right Deposits

Power Point 85: Fuss Over Backward Cap......186

    Tim Redmond   Reversing a "Backward" Situation

Power Point 86: Healthy Habits Reduce Heart Disease......188

    Dr. Patrick Quillen   ABC's of Better Health

Power Point 87: Woman Trapped By Pig......190

    Dr. Don Colbert   Recognizing Deadly Emotions

Power Point 88: Newsboys Band Takes Arena With Them......192

    Newsboys   Understanding Your Audience

Power Point 89: A Long Ride to Harvard 194

    Khadijah Williams   The Rewards of Perserverance

Power Point 90: Hotels Face Lawsuits on Surcharges 196

    Bob Harrison   To Sue or Not to Sue

Power Point 91: Man Forgets Wife at Gas Station 198

    Michelle Harrison-Ophus   Words Can Create Opportunity

Power Point 92: Robber Steals Money From Salvation Army Kettle 200

    Don and Marlene Ostrom   Release Brings Increase

Power Point 93: Thieves Steal Family History 202

    Bob Harrison   Developing Disaster Resilience

Power Point 94: Mother Battles Gator to Save Son 204

    Bill Bright   Doing the Impossible

Power Point 95: Dead Woman Sheds Tear 206

    Cindy Harrison   A Good Report List

Power Point 96: Cancer Claims Ted Kennedy 208

    Rick Warren   Overlapping Seasons of Life

Power Point 97: New Movie Features 10-Minute Segments 210

    Sharon Cook   10-Minute Changes

Power Point 98: Chef Fired for Good Cooking 212

    Tom Peters   Quality as a Passion

Power Point 99: Prayer Makes A Difference 214

    Ruth Graham   Power of Prayer

Power Point 100: Over One Million Cars Stolen 216

    Alexander Berardi   Turning Failure Into Success

Power Point 101: Man Gives 30 Gallons of Blood 218

    Bob Harrison   Reaching Beyond One's World

End Notes 221

Preface

In less than thirty days, your life could totally change as a result of learning and applying the various increase strategies contained in this book.

It is common to find people who desire to improve their lives but don't know exactly what to do and/or how, where and when to activate their plans. Whether you are one of them, or simply want to better your life, the stories and principles in this book can give you that needed direction.

Traveling to every state in America, plus over 50 countries around the world, I have shared valuable insights about how people can break the power of limiting beliefs and embrace the "Increase Lifestyle." Oftentimes, my speaking venues have afforded me the opportunity to share the stage and visit with some of the world's top achievers. On these occasions, I have made it a point to ask questions of them and to learn the unique strategies and techniques that enabled them to enjoy the fame and influence that they were experiencing. As I share their stories in this book, many of those strategies and principles are revealed.

But first, let's go back in time and share with you a brief summary of my story as it applies to this book and you.

Years ago, I was the operator of a large Southern California auto dealership. Having engineered one of the quickest dealer sales turnarounds in Chrysler's history, I was riding high. Then, the stock market crashed and interest rates skyrocketed. This combination caused many people to delay their new car purchases. I found us having to pay almost 20 percent interest for the financing of our multi-million dollar new-car inventory of vehicles that were not selling. In a short, our income was nose-diving while debts were dramatically rising.

At that time I would have given almost anything to have known about the strategies contained between the covers of this book. Instead, I had to personally begin a desperate search for answers – real answers – that could provide me with the needed lifelines to obtain personal and financial victory.

During this crisis time, I flew to Detroit, Michigan. While there, I became acquainted with a millionaire industrialist. I discovered that this man's professional life had experienced a rapid acceleration. In a few short years, he had gone from being a machine operator to owning nine corporations. What impressed me was that while achieving this level of success, he was able to balance the various aspects of his personal life extremely well. Not only that, he was a generous giver.

I inquired to learn from him what had triggered such dramatic changes. He then told me about a book that he had read and studied that was the foundation of his life-change. He said that this book had "the greatest 'principles of increase' ever written." To my amazement, I discovered that he was talking about the Bible. I had always thought of the Bible mainly as a book of theology. Now a successful businessman was telling me that it was also a handbook full of personal and financial strategies for victorious living.

Over the next several months, I examined this book to learn more about these strategies. I also began an intensive audio listening program and read numerous books about success and prosperity.

By activating my newly acquired knowledge with my business acumen, my financial situation soon began to experience a turnaround. Not only did my finances improve, but I became a more positive and joyful person. In addition, fresh love rose up from within me for my wife, children and those around me. And that is not all. Because my beliefs now had a more solid foundation, I experienced a spiritual renewal. With my values and priorities clarified, my life to took on new meaning and vibrancy.

Over the next few years I read scores of additional books and interviewed numerous achievers from all walks of life to learn their increase secrets. In the process I collected thousands of quotes on various subjects and organized them using a unique computerized retrieval system.

From across the globe, business organizations, marketing groups and churches asked me to come and share my valuable knowledge. As people heard and applied these strategies, many of them began to experience dramatic changes in their businesses and personal lives. I have received thousands of remarkable testimonials and praise reports such as the following:

A top-level network marketing distributor called excitedly exclaimed.... "This teaching has changed my life."

A businessman from the state of Washington told me... "In the last year, my income has gone from $25,000 to $140,000."

Another businessman from Oklahoma sent this extraordinary report: "Since the middle of the year my business has more than doubled. I have gotten more involved in my church. My marriage has never been happier; my wife and I are acting like two teenagers in love. I've been totally cured of cancer and I've lost seventy-five pounds."

A pastor in California phoned me and said.... "After you shared the principles of increase with our congregation, within 24 hours, more than thirty-five members had breakthroughs with their finances."

Because of dramatic changes such as these that were taking place in people's lives, the door to the speaking arena flew open even wider. Soon I was speaking at some of the world's largest success seminars and conferences, standing before audiences of up to 20,000 people and sharing the stage with many of the world's most famous achievers. In addition, I was in demand as a teacher at seminars that charged tuitions up to five-thousand-dollars-a-person. Also, I began to be invited to appear on numerous radio talk shows and national television programs—all because of the strategies that are revealed in this book!

Around this time, I noticed an unusual thing happening to me as I would read articles in newspapers. I found myself automatically thinking about a principle or strategy I had learned as it might apply to that particular incident. As I began to incorporate some of these examples into my teachings, I discovered that it helped people to understand and better remember the principles. Therefore, when I compiled this book, I decided to use different news headlines as the starting point or illustration for each featured life principle.

Many of the Power Points center around interesting or amusing incidents from my life or the lives of famous achievers. From these anecdotes, you will learn how I, and others, personally used a particular strategy or principle in their life.

As an added feature, at the conclusion of each Power Point, you are challenged to apply what you have read into your life in a specific way. Let your imagination soar as you answer the questions which are posed to jog your thinking and release fresh creativity.

For further assistance, a verse of Scripture is quoted to provide a biblical foundation for the increase principle set forth.

Finally, let me share why I chose the title *Power Points for Increase*. As it applies to this book, the word Power can be defined as: "The basic energy needed to initiate and sustain action, enabling one to translate intention into reality." It is a quality without which people cannot change and leaders cannot lead. A Point is defined as: "An exact spot, location, or time." Why does that matter to you? Because the reading of this book could be your Power Point: time to release new direction and power into your life.

Why settle for mere survival when you can live a life of victory and significance? By activating the strategies, principles and suggested actions contained within the following pages, you can experience greater achievements, rekindle love, enjoy a spiritual renewal, and/or awaken fresh creativity.

Determine to become all that you desire and all that God created you to be. Get ready for a life full of excitement and a brand-new sense of purpose. You have so much to look forward to!

Power Point Question

What could learning and activating the principles in this book do for your future?

"He…giveth power unto his people."
—Psalm 68:35

Power Points
for
Increase

BOB HARRISON

News Headline

Massive Chrysler Shutdown

Chrysler announced that it will shut down all 30 of its North American factories for a month or more and will indefinitely lay-off over 10% of its employees.

Years ago, when I read the above headline my heart sank. It had been only ten months since I had taken over as general manager of a large near-bankrupt Chrysler dealership in Orange County, California. That had been a difficult time as automotive manufactures were experiencing a major sales slump. Across the country, dealerships by the score were forced to close.

However, by applying some innovative cutting-edge strategies, I had been able to engineer a sales increase at our store of over 300%. In fact, in 90 days time the dealership had gone from the brink of closing to becoming one of Southern California's "Top Ten" Chrysler dealerships. Then the following month I had made an offer to purchase the business.

Now, after mounting that incredible comeback in sales, and then taking ownership of the store, I was faced with the prospect of my only supplier going bankrupt.

The headline froze me in my tracks. I thought, "Who is going to buy a new vehicle made by a manufacturer that might be going under? Was this shutdown going to put my business in bankruptcy? What was I going to do?"

Then one evening as I was reading in the Bible, I felt impressed to turn to the story about a prophet named Elijah in I Kings 17. One day he faced a similar crisis. Because of a famine that had gripped the land, his normal sources of supply had dried up.

In response to that dilemma, God directed him to discover a new source: a brook. He also commanded ravens to bring him food in order to sustain him through the harsh season.

As I read I thought, "My supplier is going through a sales famine. Maybe I can respond as the prophet did and find an additional source of economic nourishment." As I pondered on my situation, I realized that by contract I could only sell new cars made by Chrysler. On the other hand, I could sell any brand of used cars. If I could increase my used-car sales, then the extra income from those transactions could sustain me through the new-car meltdown.

A few days later I went to a wholesale auto auction and purchased a bundle of used Toyotas, Nissans and Hondas, plus some good-selling, American-made vehicles. Those vehicles immediately began to sell and generated much needed income.

Power Point

"What appears to be the ending might really be a fresh beginning"

–Bob Harrison

By instituting that one change, we made it through that dry economic season. Within a few months, Chrysler new-car sales started to rebound and our situation stabilized.

Since that time, when I hear from people that their principal revenue flow has been eliminated or is diminishing, I encourage them to look for different possible sources of supply.

Many of them have done this, survived, and even flourished. Many have started a second business, while some have gotten involved in real estate investments. Others have launched themselves into network marketing. One businessman friend in Arizona really got innovative. He was laid-off from his six-figure upper management job and had been unable to find work. He got the idea of buying discounted sale items at a local clearance store and then reselling the merchandise on-line. He informed me that this new revenue source was making him almost $100,000 a year.

If you are going through a season of economic famine, I would suggest that you consider the possible options for fresh sources of supply. In the words of noted television instructor Jentzen Franklin, "Sometimes the blessing of God requires us go to a different place."[1]

Power Point Question

Is there a new brook waiting for you to arrive?

"Thou shalt drink of the brook."
—I Kings 17:4

News Headline

EXTRA! EXTRA!

Final Edition

Wrong House Raided

A dozen armed police officers knocked down the front door of an elderly couple's home. They held them at gun point while they searched the residence for drugs.

The police found no drugs in the home. Later, it was discovered that the lead officer had inadvertently written down the wrong address. Charging into the wrong place is the kind of situation that Colin Powell has sought to avoid in life and when dealing with other nations. Powell, America's former secretary of state, has held many leadership positions in which judicious decision-making has been essential. When he was chairman of the Joint Chiefs of Staff, he was known for how carefully he prepared for battles. He would reportedly order satellite photos, send out scouting patrols, and collect all the intelligence available before deciding where—or whether—to attack.

COLIN POWELL'S DECISION-MAKING STRATEGY

General Powell, some friends, and I had dinner in Indianapolis immediately following a success seminar. I was impressed with how alert, articulate, and informed he was. However, he revealed something about his decision-making process that surprised me. He told me that if, "after collecting all the information that was available, a course of action was still uncertain - and if a decision did not have to be made - then I would wait. Time would often sort things out."

One of the most important characteristics of leaders and achievers is decisiveness: the ability to make tough decisions quickly. Sometimes, the delaying of decisions can create uncertainty and result in missed opportunities. On the other hand, what General Powell is saying is that there are times when deciding too quickly can lead to disastrous consequences.

I have learned this to be true through my own life experiences. If I do not have all the facts and/or do not sense an inner peace, unless a decision is required immediately, I normally delay the decision.

THE ADVANTAGES OF FLEXIBILITY

Here are some advantages of this strategy: Until I commit to a decision, I retain the ability to change, adjust, modify, or explore other options. This flexibility enables me to discover better solutions, receive more favorable terms, avoid costly mistakes, and/or tremendously increase the impact of the right decision because of better timing.

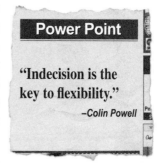

Power Point

"Indecision is the key to flexibility."

–Colin Powell

Rudolph Giuliani, the former mayor of New York City, uses the same decision-making mindset. He says, "Many are tempted to decide an issue simply to end the discomfort of indecision. However, the longer you take to make a decision, the more mature and well-reasoned it will be. I never make up my mind until I have to."[1]

Donald Trump also uses this approach in decision making. "I ask and I ask and I ask until I begin to get a gut feeling about it.....and that is when I make my decision."[2]

Particularly when making big decisions, this decision-making strategy is worth considering. Remember—great leaders are not always the ones who make the quickest decisions, but the ones who make the right decisions.

Power Point Question

Are you losing flexibility and/or making costly mistakes by forcing yourself to make some decisions too soon?

"There is a way that seemeth right unto a man, but the end thereof are the ways of death."
—Proverbs 16:2

The primary purpose of a door is to provide entrance and exit. However, if it opens at the wrong time—as happened on this flight as it was leaving Chicago—it can cause real problems. This is true not only on airliners, but also at the office or at home. Let me illustrate by explaining a problem that my friend Dick Withnell had with the open door to his office.

ARE "OPEN DOORS" YOUR PROBLEM?

Dick is a very successful Dodge dealer in the Northwest. Several years ago, I was visiting him at his dealership. During the course of our conversation, he mentioned to me that his business sales volume and income had greatly increased over the past few years. However, even though he was excited about the positive changes, he was actually feeling greater stress and having a more difficult time focusing on important tasks. He asked me for suggestions about what could he do.

I decided to observe how he was handling the flow of information and people that came to him. It soon became obvious to me that one of his main problems was the door to his office. It was located directly off a public hallway. Employees, customers, and solicitors could enter and leave through the door to his office at will.

Although Dick's desire to be accessible was admirable, his "open-door policy" gave him no control over interruptions and distractions. Sometimes, his office seemed as busy as New York's Grand Central Station during rush hour. The continued interruptions were robbing him of the privacy that is necessary for creative thinking, long-term planning, and meaningful conversations.

I advised him to remain "touchable" but to take control of interruptions. I also assured him that no one should be offended by this action if he remained accessible.

He activated my recommendation by moving his secretary's office next to his, installing a door in the wall between the two offices and giving her the open door adjacent to the hallway. He still remained accessible, but now she served as his gatekeeper. She answered the phones and made first contact with customers and employees. As a result, his stress level went down and his productivity went back up.

Power Point

"Lost time is never found again."

—*Benjamin Franklin*

ADOPT A "SCREEN-DOOR" POLICY

If you want to be truly successful and effective, you must maintain mastery of your time. In particular, you must control interruptions. The strategy is this: Whenever possible, instead of having an open-door policy, adopt a "screen-door policy." Screen your calls and guests so that you can prioritize your responsibilities and maximize your time.

Power Point Question

Who is in control of your "doors"—you or others?

—————

"No one can come into the inner court except
with the king's permission."
—Esther 4:11 (author's paraphrase)

News Headline

EXTRA! EXTRA!

Final Edition

Nails Removed From Man's Head

A carpenter stumbled on scaffolding and fell onto a coworker who was using a nail gun. As the two fell to the ground, the man's nail gun began to fire, hitting the other carpenter six times in the head. Over several days of operations, doctors were able to remove all the nails.

In order to avoid a fatal infection, the nails in this man's head had to be removed. There is a different kind of "infection" that can set into churches, clubs, businesses, and families—and it may also be "fatal." It is the negative attitude of an employee or member.

This kind of infection normally begins when someone within the organization, group, or relationship becomes upset by some other member's actions or a perceived injustice. Instead of giving the situation time to change or correct itself, the disgruntled individual begins to manifest his or her negative feelings through criticism, disrespect, pouting, temper tantrums, or hostility.

If not handled quickly and properly, this negative attitude can spread to others in the group, business, or family. If left untreated, this "infection" can be harmful to harmony.

Best-selling author John Maxwell teaches, "What starts as a bad attitude in one or two people can make a mess of the situation for everyone. Bad attitudes must be addressed. They will always cause dissension, resentment, combativeness, and division. And they will never go away on their own. They will simply fester and ruin the team."[1] He also says, "If you leave a bad apple in a barrel of good apples, you will always end up with a barrel of rotten apples."[2]

In dealing with these negative-attitude situations, consider the following strategies:

INFECTION PREVENTION KEYS

1. BE PROACTIVE: If you discover that someone is upset or negative, deal with the situation as quickly as possible.

2. GO TO THE SOURCE: Try to discover the root cause and attempt to deal with it rather than just reacting to the symptoms that are being manifested.

3. COUNTERACT THE NEGATIVE: Discuss the positive aspects of the situation or give a different point of view to the person.

4. CONTAIN THE OUTBREAK: Recognize negativism as a contagious infection that needs to be treated while it is still localized and has not spread to others.

5. PERFORM SURGERY: If the above avenues fail to correct the situation, make the changes needed to cut out the cause or carrier of the negativism.

Determine that you are not going to ignore negativism. Deal with it in a firm but compassionate manner before it infects others.

As John Maxwell states, "If you want outstanding results, then you need good people with great talents and awesome attitudes."[3]

Power Point Question

Do you have a negative-attitude situation you need to deal with?

"Now I beseech you, brethren, mark them which cause divisions."
Romans 16:17

Power Point #5

News Headline

Giuliani Starts Investment Firm

Hoping to become a big player on Wall Street, the former mayor of New York launches his own investment firm.

Since leaving the mayor's office, Rudolph Giuliani has built a successful consulting business. He and his staff help firms and governments solve critical strategic issues primarily in the areas of security and leadership. Giuliani also is a frequent speaker to corporate groups and at America's largest success seminars.

Giuliani's ability to lead was manifested by how effectively he handled the events surrounding the crisis of September 11, 2001. It was also revealed by the positive changes that he instituted in New York City prior to that event during his term as mayor, beginning in 1994.

One indication of the positive changes that transpired during Giuliani's time as mayor was a reduction in crime. The number of homicides per year nosedived from 1,946 to 642 – a drop of 67 percent. Overall, crime was reduced by some 5,000 felonies per week.[1]

In the September 1990 issue of Time magazine, the feature article was entitled "The Rotting of the Big Apple." The story described New York City as a place with vanishing jobs, crumbling infrastructure, and soaring crime. It referred to the city as "the crime and welfare capital of America." Ten years later, the cover of Time featured New York City again. This time, the magazine called it "the safest large city in America."[2]

Giuliani says, "Leadership does not just happen. It can be learned, developed, and taught." He believes that there are many ways to lead, such as by example, by inspiring with stirring speeches, and/or by strength and consistency of character."[3]

Power Points for Increase

Several friends and I dined and visited Mayor Giuliani in Anaheim, California. One of his leadership characteristics, which really impressed me, was his concept of "starting small with success."

STARTING SMALL WITH SUCCESS

When tackling big problems, Giuliani would normally find and begin with some small thing that could be could be done quickly and noticeably.

For instance, when tackling the city's crime problem, he knew that it would take time to show results but that people needed to see some improvements soon. He decided to concentrate on two areas that could be changed relatively easily and that the public would notice. The first was attacking graffiti, which was a challenge for the whole city. He devised a program that quickly eliminated graffiti from subway cars, buses and sanitation trucks. He then went after the "squeegee washers" – men who would rush up to vehicles stopped at traffic lights and tunnel entrances, spray the windshields, wipe them with a dirty rag or something, and then demand payment for their "services." These operators were notably aggressive and many drivers felt intimidated by them. Giuliani had the police issue citations against them for jaywalking, the washers were soon gone. New Yorkers loved it, and so did all the visitors who frequented the city.[4]

Power Point

"Small successes can change people's feelings and...boost morale."
– *Rudolph Giuliani*

Giuliani stated, "Small successes can change people's feelings and can, in themselves, boost morale."

Power Point Question

What big task can you start by creating small successes?

"You have been faithful with a few things;
I will put you in charge of many things."
Matt 25:21 (NIV)

News Headline EXTRA! EXTRA!

Final Edition

Last Pontiac Rolls Off Line

Ending a history of over 100 years for the brand, the final Pontiac automobile rolled off the assembly line in Michigan.

What is the best way to handle change when it involves the end of something? While at dinner one night with retired General Norman Schwarzkopf, I learned a great strategy regarding this aspect of life.

The commander of American troops for American's first war with Iraq joined some friends and I for dinner in St. Louis. I asked him, since he had retired and was an in-demand motivational speaker, if he missed being in the military. He replied, "I miss the camaraderie with the troops and the rich relationships that I had in the military, but I am greatly enjoying my new life."

Then the general stated, "One of my secrets of success in life is this: I believe that most situations in life are temporary and that...life is a collection of seasons."

A COLLECTION OF SEASONS

What a simple but powerful way to view life as revolving around seasons. The changing of weather seasons determines when the farmer plants, waters, and takes in the harvest. Season changes also dictate what kinds of clothes a mother purchases for her children and whether a vacationer heads for the mountain slopes for snow skiing or to a mountain lake for waterskiing.

Likewise, during the course of our lives, a change of careers, relationships, competitive products, or even physical capabilities can require a change of actions, obligations, and responses. Life is really a series of beginnings and endings that often require different goals, activities, resources, and relationships.

General Schwarzkopf went on to say, "Losers and victims try to hang on to a season after it is over. Winners and achievers cherish the memories and experiences of the old season but embrace the new season that is ahead."[1]

This concept of life being a collection of seasons greatly helped me when my first wife, Cindy, unexpectedly passed away in her prime. We had enjoyed many wonderful times together. However, I had to acknowledge that the season of us sharing our lives together was over. Although I would miss her, I needed to embrace my new season of being single. I realized that the sooner that I adjusted to this reality, the better dad I would be to my children, and the more capable I would be in impacting the lives of others.

Power Point

"Life is a collection of seasons."[1]

—General Norman Schwarzkopf, USA Retired

I never thought that my season of singleness would last so long. However, because I embraced that time, it became a great period of personal growth. Now, I am enjoying yet another season married to an incredible lady, Sharon.

The writer Henry David Thoreau gave this advice: "Live in each season as it passes; breathe the air, drink the water, taste the fruit, and [enjoy] the influences of each."[1]

Learn to recognize when seasons are changing and make adjustments accordingly. You will reduce stress, release fresh increase, and have a jump start on the future when you flow with the changing seasons of life.

Power Point Question

What can you do to bring "seasonal thinking" into your life?

"To everything there is a season."
—Ecclesiastes 3:1

News Headline

Teen Surfs After Shark Attack

Hawaii's number one amateur surfer remained unshaken and continued to surf following a vicious attack by a 13-foot, 1,500 pound shark.

The shark that attacked thirteen-year-old Bethany Hamilton took a 17-inch-wide bite out of her surfboard as it also bit off her arm just below the shoulder. The teenager lost more than half her blood.

Despite the gravity of her injury, Bethany refused to let this tragic incident get her down. Just ten weeks after the attack, she returned to competition at a National Scholastic Surfing Association meet. She came in fifth place for her age category.[1] Since then, she has shared her inspiring story of overcoming a tragic loss on *Oprah, 20/20, Good Morning America, Entertainment Tonight,* and *Inside Edition.*[2]

Bethany's experience is an example of how unexpected setbacks and misfortunes may suddenly appear, seemingly out of nowhere. This precious girl demonstrates the "bounce back" attitude that one must have in order to continue experiencing a life of meaning and fulfillment.

In response to negative occurrences, many times people take a "victim" viewpoint. This perspective is based upon the belief "Something is being done—or has been done—to me that has left me permanently wounded and/or powerless to overcome."

THE PRICE OF HAVING A VICTIM OUTLOOK

As my friend and superachiever mentor, Brian Klemmer, teaches, "There is a huge price to pay for living life as a victim. You may discover that your life is stalled out. You may find yourself unable to fulfill your true potential or achieve the things that matter most to you in life. Add to that a lack of respect from others, and it makes living for this victim viewpoint very costly."

So how can we avoid or come out of this negative approach to negative incidents? According to Brian, one strategy is this: "Look at the costs of living life as a victim, not only to you, but also to all the lives of those you touch. Bad things can happen to good people. How we decided to respond to those events makes all the difference in the world."

Brian suggests taking the approach that Bethany chose for herself. Focus on what you still have, not on what you have lost. As you continually place your attention and energies on what remains, soon fresh enthusiasm and joy can come forth from within, and new dreams will emerge. For instance, Bethany's friends say that she "shows off what remains of her arm."[3]

Power Point

"Bad things can happen to good people."

Brian Klemmer

Educator and author, Booker T. Washington, who was born into slavery but later lived a life of influence and meaning says, "Success is to be measured... by the obstacles which [one] has overcome."

Don't let accidents, past failures, or deep emotional hurts limit your life and stifle your future. Make a determination now to move beyond them and embrace the good life that is awaiting you.

Power Point Question

How can you better respond to negative setbacks?

"If anything is excellent or praiseworthy—think about such things."
—Philippians 4:8 (NIV)

News Headline

Final Edition

EXTRA! EXTRA!

Zig Ziglar Receives Award

Zig Ziglar has been named as recipient of the American Inspirations Award. The award is presented to a person whose faith in public life serves as an inspiration to all Americans.

Zig Ziglar is one of the world's best known sales trainers and motivational speakers. He has written ten best-selling books.

Throughout his life, Ziglar has received numerous awards. He has been recognized on three different occasions in the Congressional Record of the United States for, among other things, "contributions made to elevating sales as a profession" and "his work with youth in the drug war."

Ziglar teaches that "success means doing the best we can with what we have. Success is in the doing, not the getting; in the trying, not the triumph. [It] is a personal standard, reaching for the highest that is in us, becoming all that we can be."[1]

Zig and I have shared the speaking stage together from Honolulu to Miami and numerous cities in between. From our times together, here are some of...

ZIG ZIGLAR'S POWER POINTS

• You are what you are and where you are because of what goes in your mind.

• Regardless of your past, tomorrow is a clean slate.

• You can learn almost anything while driving in your vehicle.

• It is not what you have, but what you use, that makes the difference.

• If you do the things you ought to do when you ought to do them, the day will come when you can do the things you want to do when you want to do them.

- Sometimes adversity is what you must face in order to become successful.

- Every choice you make has an end result.

- You were designed for accomplishment, engineered for success, and endowed with seeds of greatness.

Power Point

"If you don't like the output, then change the input."
–Zig Ziglar

- The greatest enemy of excellence is good.

- When you are tough on yourself, life is easier on you.

- For motivation to be permanent, one must have balance in one's life.

- Joy is the bonus you get when you put it all together.

- Where you start is not nearly as important as where you finish.

- Failure is a detour, not a dead-end street.

- If you don't like your output, then change your input.

Zig believes that, "persistent effort, supported by a character-based foundation, enables one to get more of the things money can buy, plus all of the things money can't buy."[2]

Power Point Question

What input can you add to your life that will help you to achieve greater success?

_____

"A wise man will hear, and will increase learning."
—Proverbs 1:5

This program has been referred to as the "eye that never sleeps." A government agency might never sleep, but if you do not get enough rest, it could have serious negative effects – not only on your health, but also on your relationships and finances.

"THE SILENT CANCER"

T.D. Jakes calls fatigue "the silent cancer." Jakes is a nationally acclaimed author and megachurch pastor in Dallas, Texas. He often addresses this issue in his conferences and on his national television broadcasts. He teaches that "fatigue... robs [people] of creativity and secretly steals their energy and discernment. Tired people are...less careful. Even simple problems seem insurmountable. When fatigue robs people of their better judgment, they make permanent decisions based on the stress of temporary circumstances. Oftentimes these people are hard to work for and hard to love."[1]

Best-selling author Laurie Beth Jones concurs: "Leaders must be aware that their energy is subject to depletion and they must make guarding that energy reserve a priority."[2]

Bill Hybels, megachurch pastor and seminar speaker from the Chicago area, also warns of the danger of fatigue. He says, "Not only are physically run-down people short on energy, but they tend to be easily irritated, critical, defensive, and negative. It is hard for them to love others, and it is equally hard for others to love them."[3]

Richard Exley, who is a best-selling author and a friend of mine, says, "Don't deceive yourself. Rest is not optional...in Old Testament times, Sabbath-breakers were executed."[4]

Real estate mogul Donald Trump also believes in the need for rest. He says, "To be successful, it is not enough to have brains; you must have the energy. The true deal people sleep at night no matter what."[5]

Norvel Hayes, a multimillionaire investor and successful seminar speaker, told me something about rest twenty years ago that I have never forgotten. He said that often he could help people get out of depression and/or negativity just by getting them to take a break and rest. He exclaimed, "Tired people lean towards problems; rested people lean toward answers!"

> **Power Point**
>
> **"Fatigue robs people of their better judgment."**
>
> *–T.D. Jakes*

Jakes teaches that, "Even soil must be allowed time to lie fallow in order that its nutrients and minerals will be replenished. Only then can it return with a healthy crop that lives up to its full potential."[6]

If you have been pushing yourself or others too hard, why not stop the pace? Take a nap, go to bed early, enjoy a dinner without your cell phone, and/or escape—without your lap top—for a long weekend.

Power Point Question

What can you do to break the cycle of fatigue and empower yourself?

"There remaineth therefore a rest to the people of God."
—Hebrews. 4:9

Anthony Robbins and some of his friends were in New York City. They needed a van—not for a year but for an afternoon. They desired to deliver meals and gifts to needy families on Thanksgiving Day. The only problem was it was a holiday weekend and all the rental places were either out of vans or closed. Then Anthony got an idea.

I was visiting one of his seminars in Chicago when he shared this inspirational story about perseverance. Anthony turned to his friends and boldly said, "Look, the bottom line is this: If we want something bad enough, we can make it happen! All we have to do is begin to take action. The problem is not that there are no vans in New York City. The only problem is that we don't have one."

Fresh with that awareness, the group determined to get a van. First, they tried walking out in front of vans that were driving down the street. Although they waved their hands, the drivers not only didn't stop, they swerved around them and sped up.

Then they tried waiting by a traffic light. When a van would stop for a red light, one of them would walk over and say, "Today is Thanksgiving. We'd like to help some needy families. Would you drive us to a certain underprivileged area here in New York City?" No one they asked was willing to do that.

Then they tried offering the different drivers $100 to transport them. That got people's attention. However, when the drivers were told the area where the members wanted to go, they all said no.

PERSEVERING THROUGH NEGATIVE RESPONSES

Robbins' friends were about ready to give up when he exclaimed, "It's the law of averages: Sooner or later, somebody is going to say yes."

Shortly hereafter, another van drove up to the traffic light where the group was standing. It was extra big and could accommodate all of them. When they asked the driver to help them, he said, "I'd be happy to take you." He reached over, grabbed a cap, and put it on his head. They were all astonished when they noticed what was written on it: "Salvation Army."

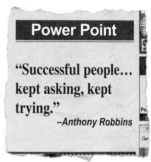

Power Point

"Successful people... kept asking, kept trying."
–Anthony Robbins

The man drove them to a grocery store, and then they all went out and spent the afternoon blessing people.

This story is a good illustration of not giving up in the face of negative responses.

Sales Trainer Tom Hopkins also teaches this concept in his seminars: "A person is not judged by the number of times that they fail but by the times they succeed. Success then is in direct proportion to the number of times that one fails but keeps on trying."[2]

Robbins teaches that oftentimes the key to overcoming adversity is to think like martial arts experts. Their goal is not to meet force with force, but rather to guide it in a new direction.[3]

Power Point Question

What shortages or obstacles have been preventing you from a desired outcome?

"Why stand ye gazing?"
—Acts 1:11

News Headline

Survival Attitude Helps Downed Pilot

An American pilot survived five days in enemy territory after bailing out of his jet.

After his jet was hit by a surface-to-air missile, Captain Scott O'Grady ejected and parachuted to the ground. He then raced into the woods. Equipped with a survival pamphlet, radio, first-aid kit, distress flares, and a compass, he was able to survive for five days in hostile conditions by living on rainwater, wild plants, and bugs. Captain O'Grady "put to good use the lessons learned during 17 days of… training he had undertaken" at the Air Force's Survival school.[1]

At this school, his instructors did not just teach survival skills, but also a survival attitude.

What is a survival attitude? It is a force inside people that enables them to rise up, bounce back, and even triumph in the face of negative circumstances. Normally, a survival attitude is not something that a person is born with; it is a learned behavior. It can be acquired from family or friends who have that attitude, it can be taught through actual training, or developed by experiences in the marketplace of life.

DEVELOPING A SURVIVAL ATTITUDE

A great example of a person who developed this vital life skill through life experience is Dexter Yager. Dexter and his wife, Birdie, operate the largest network marketing organization in the world. I have been privileged to speak with them on several occasions. He likes to share how he developed the survival attitude when he was a child.

"While in the sixth grade, I wanted to make some extra money. There were several construction people working on a project in the area. There were no vending machines nearby, and the workers couldn't take off work to visit stores.

"I got the idea of buying soda pop for five cents a bottle, and then turning around and selling them for a dime. I could use the ice from my mother's refrigerator to keep the bottles cold.

"I began. Immediately, my business was a great success. Soon I was selling cases and cases of pop. I was earning more money than many adults.

"Some vendors learned of my success and came in with their own ice and drinks. They were much bigger than me. I knew that if I wanted to keep my business, I had to fight back. That's what I did. I hired some kids to help me. We offered more drinks for the price and added different flavors so that we had a better selection. And on hot days, we made sure we never ran out of ice!

"We won the battle. Our competition went away. For them, it was just another business, but to me, it was a dream come true."[2]

A person begins to develop a survival attitude when he or she resists the urge to quit and instead fights back. Each action helps to form a habit, and habits create attitudes.

Power Point Question

What steps can you take to form the habit of resisting adversity?

"Though I walk in the midst of trouble, you preserve [me]."
—Psalms 138:7 (NIV)

> **Power Point**
>
> **"Things do not change until you don't quit."**
> —*Dexter Yager*

Police chiefs in the United Kingdom are considering replacing the familiar 12-inch tall helmet with new head gear that looks like a bicycle helmet and can withstand a blow from a baseball bat. The decision to change the headgear of England's bobbies is not an easy one. The British love tradition. However, their police also have an appreciation for defensive armament.

Because England is an island country that has been attacked many times, the leadership of the country also has an appreciation for the defensive mind-set. This fact became quite evident to me during a lunchtime conversation I had with Great Britain's former prime minister Margaret Thatcher.

A DEFENSIVE-PROTECTION MIND-SET

Lady Thatcher, Britain's first female prime minister, is a very charming, bright, and articulate woman. During her time in office, her nation began to rebound economically as state-owned companies and government-furnished rental homes were replaced with private ownership.

Also, during her tenure, Britain started to regain its tarnished reputation as a world power. Her defensive mind-set became clear to me when she said, "It is only with strong defenses that freedom can be maintained. Evil and conflict will always be with us, and so we must keep our defenses strong."

She went on to say, "For every offensive weapon that your enemy possesses, you must have a defensive counterpart or you will eventually be defeated."

From my time with her, here are more of Lady Thatcher's insightful thoughts:

INSIGHTFUL THOUGHTS FROM MARGARET THATCHER

- STRENGTH: "A bully has no respect for a weakling .The only way to stop a bully is not to be weak."

- HOME: "It can be a base of operations, but it must also be a refuge."

Power Point

"We must keep our defenses strong."

—Lady Margaret Thatcher

- GOVERNMENT: "When a government allows its people and enterprises to flourish, then the country will flourish."

- ECONOMICS: "The way to recovery is through profits."

- FREEDOM: "You cannot have freedom without laws, rules, and responsibilities."

- OPPOSITION: "Sometimes you must be more concerned about the knives at your back than the guns in front of you."

- BATTLES: "You may have to fight a battle more than once to win it."

- PERSONAL ATTACKS: "People can be vicious. Don't pay too much attention to them or you will get a complex about yourself."

- ACHIEVING: "It is easy to begin a job, but a lot harder to see it through."

- SPIRITUALITY: "It is only in recognizing that people are spirit beings that individuals achieve importance and significance."

Power Point Question

In what ways would increasing your defensive-protection mind-set change your decisions—economically, martially, physically, spiritually?

"A wise man is strong."
—Proverbs 24:5

News Headline

Final Edition

EXTRA! EXTRA!

Resort Town Bans Ties

Declaring that ties are detrimental to the resort image of the island, a city located on the Gulf of Mexico has approved a resolution banning them.

If you are tired of wearing ties, then South Padre Island, Texas might be a place you want to be. And if you are weary of ending up tied in sports contests and/or in business, then better preparation might be your answer.

Experts agree that one of the best ways to improve the odds for positive outcomes is through increased preparation. A good example of how superior preparation opened the door of opportunity may be found in the life of Mary Lou Retton.

Mary Lou is as exciting and vibrant in person as she was in the 1984 when, at the Summer Olympic Games, she won five medals. Those who watched, will never forget her perfect score of 10 in the final event of gymnastics competition . In doing so, she became the first American ever to win an individual gymnastics gold medal.

Today, Mary Lou is a popular seminar speaker. We visited backstage during a seminar in Tampa, Florida, where she was speaking. She told me that proper preparation is one of her secrets to success—in gymnastics, in the speaking arena, and in life. In fact, being prepared helped her get her start. She said, "I knew that I had to be the best in practice or I would not be the best in competition."

At the seminar, she shared how preparation also supplied her "big break": "One of my teammates was injured before an international meet. The coach turned to me and said, 'Retton, you're in.' Because I was ready for that moment, I was on the team from that day on."

Here are what some other superachievers have said about the importance of preparation.

ARE YOU READY?

"Talent alone will not make you a success. Neither will being at the right place at the right time, unless you are ready. The important question is, 'Are you ready?'" —Johnny Carson[1]

"Games may be played in a stadium, but they are won or lost on the practice field." —NFL head coach Joe Gibbs[2]

"Success occurs when opportunity meets preparation." —Zig Ziglar[3]

"The will to win is important, but what is more important is the will to prepare to win."

—College basketball head coach Bobby Knight[4]

"Good fortune is what happens when opportunity meets with preparation."

—Thomas Edison[5]

"Before everything else, being ready is the secret of success."

—Henry Ford[6]

"Preparation is the single most important ingredient to success."

—Rudolph Giuliani[7]

> **Power Point**
>
> **"I had to be the best in practice or I would not be the best in competition."**
>
> *—Mary Lou Retton*

Power Point Question

How prepared are you for the position or dream that you desire?

———————————

"Thou hast been faithful over a few things,
I will make thee ruler over many things."
—Matthew 25:21

Power Point #14

News Headline

Final Edition

EXTRA! EXTRA!

Collision With Pole Restores Eyesight

The sudden restoration of a 63-year-old man's sight took place at a shopping mall when he accidentally walked into a pole.

A childhood accident had caused him to lose his sight in one eye. The sudden jolt apparently dislodged the damaged lens that had been blocking his vision for years.

A pole also changed the course of Jerome Edmondson's life. It was not one that he walked into, however, but one that he found.

As a young teenager, Jerome Edmondson determined that he was not going live in poverty. When he told his grandmother that he wanted more from his life than that, she said, "Well, son, what are you going to do?" He replied, "I'm going to play basketball."

Jerome knew that his grandmother could not afford a basketball pole and hoop, so it seemed as if there was no way he could practice and achieve his desire.

Jerome shares, "At about that same time, a storm blew through our little town. The high winds broke a big electricity pole and knocked it down. I immediately got a chain, wrapped it around the pole, and started dragging. It took me all day to get that pole home.

"I cut the pole in half with a handsaw. Then I dug a deep hole and tried to lift the pole. A farmer happened to drive by. When I shared my dream, he went and got his tractor and lifted the pole into place.

"Finding a sheet of plywood, I nailed a section of it to the pole for my backdrop. For a rim, I got an old bicycle wheel—took out the spokes—and hammered it onto the board.

"Now, I was on my way to fulfilling my dream. Every day, before and after school, I used my new basketball hoop to practice.

"When the day for seventh grade basketball tryouts came, I tried out. To my great disappointment, I did not make the team. Nevertheless, I was not about to throw away my dream. I went back home and continued to shoot more baskets.

Power Point

"The higher you reach, the greater your success."

–Jerome Edmondson

"The following year I tried out again. This time I made the team. The next year, as a freshman, the coach asked me to play varsity on the high school team. Soon I was the best player on the team."[1]

The determination that Jerome learned as a young man set a pattern for his life. He went on to become America's first minority Denny's franchise owner and then the nation's first black A&W franchise owner. Today, he is the president of a restaurant company and speaks at seminars and conference across the globe.

Jerome calls this process of holding on to your dream and walking it out step-by-step "tenacity." He encourages people to, "Stay with your dream. The higher you reach, the greater your success."[2]

Power Point Question

Do you have a dream that you need to activate?

What I am commanding you today is not too
difficult for you or beyond your reach."
—Deuteronomy 30:11 (NIV)

News Headline

Swimmers Told Not To Spit In Pool

The United States Olympic Committee gave American athletes some helpful etiquette strategies to use during the games.

One instruction given to the swimming team was "Do not spit in the pool." Officials gave this directive because they did not want the participants to do something that would intimidate other competitors nor infuriate the fans.

Tamara Lowe had a different kind of problem by the pool one day. It happened in Hawaii where she and her husband, Peter, were scheduled to speak at one of my Increase Events. Tamara is recognized as one of the world's most successful speakers. Her book, *Get Motivated*, was a *New York Times* bestseller.

During her speaking session, she shared about the incident at the pool. "The first day that Peter and I arrived in Maui, we went out to the pool. It was a lovely day—the sun was out and a breeze was lightly blowing. While I was watching my two beautiful boys, eight-year-old Zachary and three-year-old Blaze, play around the pool, I noticed Blaze toddling over close to the edge. When he got about one step away from the pool, he pulled down his trunks. Before I could react, he started to pee in the pool!

Suddenly, people stopped talking and focused on what was happening. Some of them were shocked while others were offended. A few stared at me as if I could have prevented it.

When my son came back to me, I said to him, "Blaze, honey, do not do that. If you need to go to the bathroom, come and tell Mommy." He replied, 'And then you'll take me to the pool to go pee?' I said 'No.'"

After telling the conference attendees about this episode, Tamara stated that the point to her sharing the story was this: "You can be at a luxury resort in Hawaii, your business can be going great, you can be making a lot of money, and you can feel like a king of the earth. However, in the middle of all that, someone might unexpectedly disrupt your life by 'peeing in your pool!'"

PLAYING A BAD HAND WELL

Tamara went on to share how we cannot always control what happens to us in life. She believes that successful people are not those "chosen few" who do not experience negative occurrences. They just choose not let those negative experiences ruin their day - or their lives.

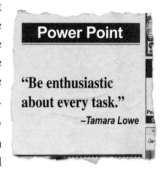

Power Point

"Be enthusiastic about every task."

–Tamara Lowe

As Motivational Speaker Dennis Waitley says, "Sometimes success in life comes not from having a good hand...but in playing a bad hand well."[1]

Tamara believes that it is critical for one to continually cultivate the attitude of a superachiever by being upbeat and positive.

If you—or someone close to you—have had an experience that has caused embarrassment or negative feelings to set in, determine today not to let the power of any situation continue to cause hurt and inaction.

Power Point Question

How will you respond to the storms of your life?

―――――――――

"If thou faint in the day of adversity, thy strength is small."
—Proverbs 24:10

News Headline

EXTRA!
EXTRA!

Final
Edition

Man Searches For Absentee Dad

A U.S. sailor who fathered a child with a Chinese dancer disappeared from their lives over half a century ago. The child, now 56, is searching for his father.

There is an inherent longing in children to connect with their parents. This man is desperate to know who his father is and, if he is still living, to have a relationship with the parent who abandoned him.

There is a different kind of missing father. He is called an "Absentee Dad."

ABSENTEE DADS

Noted author and radio commentator James Dobson illustrates this problem with a story about a four-year-old who asks his playmate, "Where is your daddy? I never see him at your house." The other boy replies, "Oh, my dad doesn't live here, he just sleeps here."[1]

The son of a prominent national minister had a tearful reunion with his father in jail. The son repented of a rebellious lifestyle and drug abuse, saying, "I've spent my whole life trying to get your attention."

So how does one respond when career and family seem to be in conflict?

A key presidential advisor at the White House walked away from his job after his ten-year-old son wrote him the following note: "Baseball's not any fun when there is no one to applaud."

Professional basketball coach Danny Ainge abruptly resigned from his prestigious job saying, "I wanted to make a statement to my family that they are more important than my career."[2]

MAKE FAMILY A PRIORITY

What these men did was right for them and their families, but success-oriented people do not need to become career-less in order to be good parents.

However, they must make family a priority.

Lee Iacocca, the former chairman of Chrysler Corporation, who literally kept the company from closing, made being a good parent a priority. When he was in town, he spent his evenings and Sundays at home with his family saying, "My job takes up enough time without my having to shortchange my children."[3] He also stated, "Of all the jobs I've had in my life, no job has been more important to me than my job as a dad. I've always felt that when I die, if I can say I've done well by my family, then I've lived a full and good life."[4]

Power Point

"No job has been more important to me than my job as a dad."
–Lee Iacocca

One strategy for being a more effective parent is to schedule family time the same way that you would schedule your business appointments.

Another important strategy is this: When you are with your family members, don't just be there physically. Be there mentally and spiritually, as well. Let them have your attention and your emotions. Get involved in their dreams, their games, and their conversations.

Even if you are a non-resident dad, the quality of the relationship you have with your children is important. Studies show that adolescents who feel that their non-resident dad loves and cares for them have a higher self-esteem, less delinquency and few depressive symptoms than those who actually live with a father but aren't close.

As Iacocca states, "Other than family, what else is there that is really important? When it is all over, you are only as good as the sharing that you have done with those around you...especially your family."[5]

Power Point Question

What priority do you REALLY place on family?

"Fathers [and mothers], do not embitter your children,
or they will become discouraged."
—Colossians 3:21

The above rare occurrence can take place if a certain anesthetic mixes with a patient's intestinal gases and accidently is ignited by a spark from electrical surgical instruments.

I have had some experience with "exploding people." However, these individuals were not in surgery. They had an anger problem and seemingly could not control their outbursts.

DON'T ALLOW ANGER TO TAKE HOLD

Anger, in itself, is neither good nor bad. It is just an emotion. Whether it is a problem or not depends upon how and where the emotion is released. Problems occur when anger is released in an unacceptable manner. Unbridled outbursts can create barriers of fear and intimidation with others, resulting in the sowing of long-lasting hurts. They can also negatively affect the health and image of the individual concerned.

For instance, I remember watching news coverage, years ago about the head football coach at a major university in the Midwest. He had an emotional outburst during which he allegedly punched a police officer. As a result, the coach was forced to resign from his prestigious job.

One strategy for dealing with anger is to find activities that allow you to "vent." Hitting a punching bag, throwing darts, swimming, taking a walk, or playing competitive sports, can release pent-up emotions.

Another strategy is to document the times that outbursts occur. If there is a frequency of displays two to four hours after mealtimes, it is possible that low blood sugar levels might be a factor. If so, a change of diet might make a big difference.

An effective strategy for dealing with anger is taught by Tim LaHaye, who is a best-selling author and in-demand speaker. In his book *Anger Is a Choice* he states that, "hurt and anger from past experiences can continue to affect us now." It could be very helpful to identify sources of hurt and anger from past experiences and deal with those root issues.[1]

Power Point

"Releasing anger through emotional outbursts is a habit."

—*Tim LaHaye*

T.D. Jakes believes that, "Since emotions are such an integral part of our lives, it is important to find safe places to release our feelings."[2]

For example, author Derek Prince wrote about a young man whose life was changed by recognizing this truth. "[The man] had carried bitterness, resentment, anger, and rebellion against his father, who had been dead for years. He [drove] several hundred miles to the cemetery where his father was buried…He knelt [at his father's grave] and, for the next several hours, emptied out all his poisonous attitudes. He did not get up until he knew he had forgiven his father…His wife testifies today that she has a brand-new husband."[3]

LaHaye teaches that "releasing anger through emotional outbursts is a habit. Habits can be broken. A person need not remain a slave to that or any other habit."[4]

If you are dealing with an anger problem, make the effort to change. You will avoid damage to your self-image and needless hurts in your relationships.

Power Point Question

In what constructive ways can you better deal with anger?

"He that ruleth his spirit [is better] than he that taketh a city."
—Proverbs 16:32

News Headline

Final Edition

EXTRA! EXTRA!

Turtle Falls From Sky, Hits Man Driving Convertible, Causes Crash, Sends Him To Hospital

A Fort Lauderdale resident, who was leisurely driving his convertible with the top down, was hit on the head with a falling object. According to police, the object that hit him was an airborne turtle.

When I read this article, I wondered how a turtle could become airborne. Well, the authorities surmised that a seagull had apparently snatched a turtle from a nearby beach. As the bird began its flight, it discovered that the turtle was too heavy to hold on to. As a result, it lost its grip and the turtle fell and hit the driver of the car.

At home or on the job, many of us face a dilemma that is similar to what this bird encountered—attempting to do and/or hold on to too much. In doing so, many times the weight of it all becomes more than we can handle, and we lose the grip on our priorities, our time, our health—even our relationships.

Noted speaker Denis Waitley tells of a time several years ago when he found himself in this state of overcommitment "with an overloaded calendar but not really building any last success...I had everything going for me...but nothing coming together. I had a house but not the home life. I had the family...but not the spiritual foundation so vital to relationships."[1]

If you feel overcommitted and under stress from trying to do too much, then read on.

GET-A-GRIP KEYS

Ruth Stafford Peale, the widow of Norman Vincent Peale, was a noted author and gifted lecturer. She and I shared the stage together at a success seminar in Little Rock, Arkansas. She was in her 80s when her husband passed away and she inherited the responsibility of a communications empire. The following are several keys to a balanced life that I learned from her.

1. KNOW YOUR PRIORITIES: Make a list of what is really important to you in the long run and review it regularly. Constantly remind yourself of what your personal priorities are.

2. TAKE THINGS AS THEY COME: Retrain your brain not to worry about the unknown. Be organized and plan ahead, but also learn to react to things as they come so that you will be better able to solve problems that arise.

3. MAKE TIME FOR RELAXATION: Don't think of relaxation time just in terms of weekends, holidays, and vacations. Each day, carve out little niches of quiet spaces to reduce the pressure, clear your mind, and become empowered.

Power Point

"Carve out little niches of quiet time to reduce the pressure...and become empowered."
—*Ruth Stafford Peale*

4. BRING GOD INTO YOUR SITUATIONS: Take time for meditation and prayer. If you seek God's guidance and receive His blessing of peace, you will be better able to handle any situation.[2]

In conclusion, do not let the extra weights of overcommitment and misplaced priorities cause you to lose your grip on what is really important in your life. In trying to hold on to and/or do too much, you—like the seagull in the above story—could risk losing something really valuable.

Power Point Question

Have you clearly defined what is and what is not important to you?

"The wisdom of the prudent is to understand his way."
—Proverbs 14:8

News Headline

EXTRA! EXTRA!

Final Edition

Swimmer Loses Trunks During Race

The choppy surf created an unexpected problem for one of the competitors at the Pensacola Bay Swim. During the race he lost his swim trunks.

After swimming in rough waters, David Mayo was embarrassed to discover that, while competing in the race, he had lost his trunks. He wouldn't climb aboard a rescue boat until he had some backup shorts.

The adversity that he had to deal with that day was nothing compared to what he had to overcome as a sixteen-year-old. One summer afternoon, while kayaking with family and friends in Idaho, David experienced a life-altering accident. He decided to climb some rock formations and, while doing so, slipped and fell fifty feet, landing backside on a boulder. Mayo told me of the accident, "At first, they did not think I was going to live."

While he was in the hospital, the doctors informed him that he had severed his spine and was paralyzed. Confined to a wheelchair, he lost all hope that he would ever be able to live a normal life again.

While we were having lunch one day, David told me that, several days after hearing the doctors' diagnosis, something happened that changed his attitude. An awareness came over him that he had been given a second chance at life. It was then he determined that being in a wheelchair was not going to dim his love for life.

David began to participate in a wide variety of athletic endeavors. Soon, he was snowboarding, and playing table tennis. Then he took up swimming, scuba diving, white-water rafting, hand cycling and tennis. Since he particularly enjoyed tennis, David decided to hire a personal coach. Winning several tournaments, he has dazzled the competition. In fact he was recently named "Florida Wheelchair Player of the Year."

David is now a successful businessman, happily married. He is living proof that adversity need not keep a person down.

"Success can be predicted by how one...responds to negative events," states Dr. Paul Stoltz in his book *Adversity Quotient*. "Those who are victimized by adversity become weaker. Those who respond to adversity as an opportunity—with a sense of purpose and a sense of control—actually may get stronger."[1]

Power Point

"Success can be predicted by how one responds to negative events."

–Paul Stoltz

Dr. Albert Bandura, a Stanford psychologist and a leading researcher on self-efficacy, affirms this thinking: "People who have a belief in their... ability to meet challenges as they arise, bounce back from failures."[2]

Life can be hard. Negative events might unexpectedly happen. How you deal with them will determine your destiny. Determine to be like David Mayo who says, "I am an eternal optimist who is always believing the best in things."[3]

Power Point Question

How can you better deal with unexpected adversity?

"If you falter in times of trouble, how small is your strength!"
—Proverbs 24:10 (NIV)

My friend Les Brown says, "When you want something so badly that you refuse to give up or let go, you will probably get it."

Of all the speakers with whom I share the stage, probably none is more alive and energetic than Les. He has the incredible ability to transfer his enthusiasm and energy to his audience. Les believes that success-oriented people possess a powerful force that enables them to overcome obstacles and live out their dreams. He calls this force "hunger"!

Hunger is a powerful determination—a consuming desire—fueled by the anticipation and excitement of a future reward. It is a mind-set that can be created, fed, and increased in intensity from whatever state or condition one may be in.

In his book *Live Your Dreams* Les states, "Wanting something is not enough. You must hunger for it. Your motivation must be absolutely compelling. Hunger will give you the courage to take your dreams and run with them."[1]

From my notes of our times together, here are some of Les Brown's hunger-increasing strategies.

HUNGER-INCREASING STRATEGIES

1. TAKE RESPONSIBILITY FOR YOUR LIFE: Stop blaming other people and past negative circumstances for where you are and what you have. It is up to you to accomplish your dreams.

2. GET AROUND SUCCESSFUL PEOPLE: Absorb their attitudes and spirits. Find out what motivates them. Observe how they are different from non-achievers.

3. READ AND LISTEN: Listen to motivational CDs or tapes and read inspirational material, such as the biographies of great people. Learn how others overcame great odds and what they did to achieve their goals.

4. OVERCOME YOUR LIMITATIONS: Don't let your fears hold you back. Unmask them and master them. Push them aside.

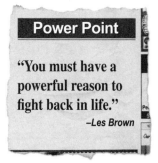

Power Point

5. VISUALIZE: Feed your subconscious. Regularly view pictures of your desired objectives.

6. DEVELOP A SENSE OF URGENCY: Take actions now that will move you toward your goals. Operate on a massive, relentless scale in order to accomplish your goals.

"You must have a powerful reason to fight back in life."

–*Les Brown*

Les believes that "with a powerful hunger for your dreams driving you, you will be surprised at the ideas that will come, the people you will be able to attract, and the opportunities that will unfold."[2]

Power Point Question

Could you be doing more to increase your hunger for success?

"Blessed are they who hunger, for they will be fed."
—Matthew 5:6 (author's paraphrase)

News Headline

EXTRA! EXTRA!

Final Edition

Cadillac Crashes Into Bedroom

A driver lost control of his vehicle, knocked over a stop sign, skidded across a lawn, and smashed into the bedroom of a woman who was asleep.

The desire for a Cadillac in her garage—not in her bedroom—changed one woman's life. It caused her to begin a frantic search for uniqueness and knowledge in order to gain her dream.

It happened in 1955. *The $64,000 Question*, a popular quiz show, was the hottest program on television. On Tuesday nights, people watched the efforts of contestants attempting to win the top prize, which was a fortune at that time.[1]

As this woman watched the show, she believed that she was smart enough to be a contestant. She did not even dream of winning the $64,000 top prize. Her goal was to win the prize given at a lower level—a new Cadillac.

However, being selected to be on the show was a challenge. All the contestants were similar in only one respect: an incongruity in their lives. For instance, there was a shoemaker who knew all about opera and a burly marine who was a gourmet cook.

She analyzed her own situation. She was short, blonde, and pretty. Se was also a psychologist and the mother of an almost three-year-old. There was nothing paradoxical about her, nothing that would catch the attention of the producers who chose the show's contestants. Then she realized that she could create her uniqueness. After much consideration, she decided upon the strategy of becoming an expert on boxing. That would be sufficiently opposite of her image to attract attention.[2]

THE POWER OF KNOWLEDGE

The woman stated, "I went to work to turn myself into a boxing expert. I ate, drank, and slept boxing; its history, its statistics, its personalities. When

I felt like I was ready, I applied to be on the show and was accepted. I went on and won. I came back and won again. I kept on winning until...I won the Cadillac."[3]

That wasn't all. She continued winning until she also won $64,000!

That event changed her life. Soon she was on television and radio programs and was making personal appearances. She was in show business and a whole new career took off![4]

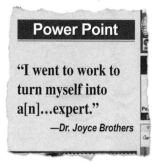

Power Point

"I went to work to turn myself into a[n]...expert."

—*Dr. Joyce Brothers*

This woman is Dr. Joyce Brothers.

Alvin Toffler said, "Knowledge...serves as a wealth and force multiplier."[5] This is true even in the sales arena. Harvey Mackay says, "The most powerful weapon anyone can possess in any negotiation is superior information and knowledge."[6]

Possessing knowledge might not win you a luxury car or cause you to be a quiz show champion, but it can release blessings and increase in your life.

Determine today to become more knowledgeable in the areas of your life where you desire increase.

Power Point Question

How much time are you actively spending on increasing your knowledge?

———————

"[God says,] My people are destroyed for lack of knowledge."
—Hosea 4:6

News Headline

Final Edition

EXTRA! EXTRA!

Governor Schwarzenegger Announces Plan

California's governor unveiled his recovery plan and called on the legislature to pass reforms so the state no longer spends more money than it receives.

Schwarzenegger knows that the state's spending will not be equal to its income unless the legislature makes balancing the budget a goal. The setting of goals causes one to focus time and energy on desired results. As admirable as this process might be, the setting of goals does not guarantee accomplishment. It only gives a government, business, or person a target.

For example, at the beginning of January, many people take time to list their goals and objectives for the coming year. With a rush of enthusiasm and fresh motivation, they excitedly dream and plan the accomplishments they anticipate in their finances and careers.

However, for many people, within weeks, this enthusiasm has diminished or has been lost altogether. A recent survey conducted in Britain said that "half of all people who make New Year resolutions break them within a month."[1] This happens because many of these plans, goals, and projects become bogged down in the "muddy marsh" of inertia. Others sink altogether in the "quicksand" of discouragement.

This result does not need to be your fate. You can greatly boost the probability of carrying out your resolutions by following these simple strategies:

STRATEGIES FOR ACHIEVING YOUR GOALS

1. BE REALISTIC: Set levels of achievement that are believable and attainable. If you succeed in achieving or going beyond these levels, that's great. Then you can set new goals.

2. DON'T SET TOO MANY: If you try to change and/or improve too many things at once, you could easily become discouraged. It is better to identify one or two deeply seated desires or needs for change and concentrate on those.

3. SET GOALS IN MULTIPLE AREAS: Don't get caught in the trap of setting only financial and career goals. Plan for increase in other areas: physical, mental, spiritual, important relationships, and giving.

4. DIVIDE INTO SMALLER STRATEGIES: Avoid being overwhelmed by large tasks. Break down your big goals into smaller units. For instance, if your goal is to lose fifty pounds in the next year, go after four pounds per month or one pound per week as your action strategy.

Power Point

"The hardest rock will yield to those who drill with determination."[2]
–Jewish Folk Saying

5. KEEP YOURSELF MOTIVATED: Do what is necessary to keep the desire for change strong. Display pictures representing your targets. Think about the benefits of succeeding. Keep positive input strong.

6. AVOID EXCUSES: Don't let misses become excuses for quitting. If you slip, then begin again.

7. PRAY: Prayer is an empowering force that can help you to break old habits.

Keep in mind that even though the creation of goals is important, it is only through sustained action that you will experience change.

Power Point Question

How can you better sustain action for reaching your goals this year?

———————

"I press toward the mark."
—Philippians 3:14

After getting what he demanded, a robber asked the bank employee to help him leave the building. He failed in his misdeed because he did not plan ahead by considering a fundamental strategy to success: In almost everything, make sure you have an exit strategy.

I first became aware of the necessity of using such a strategy when I was a nineteen-year-old college student. During the summer break, I needed a well-paying job. I settled on driving a large delivery truck for a soda company in Los Angeles.

One day, I had to make a delivery to the back of a store. The only way to get there was to drive down a narrow alley. In order to enter the alley, I had to negotiate a wide turn in the street utilizing an empty parking space.

After making the delivery, I began to back up to leave. To my horror, I saw that a car was now parked in the "empty" parking space. I was hopelessly stuck in the alley until the driver returned and moved the vehicle. It was then that I became aware of the powerful principle of having an exit strategy. This principle has helped to guide my decisions throughout my life.

HAVE AN EXIT STRATEGY!

I employ this way of thinking in many areas of my life—from learning the location of the nearest emergency exit upon checking into a hotel room to leaving maneuvering room between my vehicle and the next car when I parallel park.

I use this strategy in the business arena. Normally, before entering into a transaction, I ask myself, what will be our costs and/or options if this deal doesn't work? What is the exit strategy?

There are times when exit-strategy thinking is not necessary and may even be counterproductive. However, there are other times when it is absolutely essential. Thinking this way does not imply a sense of untrustworthiness or a lack of commitment. It merely indicates that both parties are considering all possible outcomes before beginning a binding agreement.

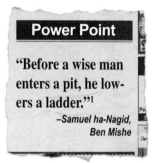

Power Point

"Before a wise man enters a pit, he lowers a ladder."[1]
–Samuel ha-Nagid, Ben Mishe

Consider your own need for better exit-strategy thinking. Using this mind-set could help you avoid needless heartaches, personal calamities, lost friendships, and vexing legal problems.

Power Point Question

How can you better make exit-strategy thinking a part of your daily life and negotiating strategy?

"He will…provide a way out."
—1 Corinthians 10:13 (NIV)

News Headline

Stocks Ignoring Bad Economic News

The market is better at accepting bad economic and corporate news, and investors are now focusing on the next earnings period in a positive manner.

Truly successful people are those who think positively and believe for good things. Even in the midst of gloomy news or the negative reports of others around them, they have trained themselves to maintain an undoubting attitude.

A DECISION ABOUT NEGATIVE REPORTS

A perfect example of such as person is Bill Swad. Bill's life changed when he made a decision not to accept a negative report.

When he decided to get out of his economic rut, Bill was a baggage handler at the Columbus, Ohio Airport. He determined to accomplish his goal by going into the used-car business. At one of my Florida Increase Events, he shared the story of his opening-day experience.

"I borrowed money from a loan company to purchase three cars, and then I rented a small lot on a busy street. After hanging some light bulbs on a wire, I was ready for business. My sales shack was like a little greenhouse made out wood and glass. However, I felt ten feet tall on the inside because I had made a total decision regarding my future, and I believed that I could do it.

"That first morning, the postman stopped by with some junk mail. He said, 'Mister, you probably ought to know that several businesses have started on this corner. Every one of them failed.'

"I wasn't about to let his negative beliefs ruin my future. I looked at the mailman and boldly exclaimed, 'Well, mister, this business is going to succeed.'"

Within three years, Bill was the biggest retail used-car dealer in the state. Next came new car dealerships. He became so successful that, at one time, he simultaneously operated the largest Chevrolet, Chrysler, and Nissan dealerships in the state of Ohio. In addition, he ran a large automobile leasing company and a finance company. Then he added an insurance company and two mortgage companies.

"An attitude is the direction in which you lean," says Lou Tice, a noted author and teacher of superachievers. "An attitude is negative, if you anticipate negative outcomes, such as pain, displeasure, embarrassment, ridicule, failure, or hurt. An attitude is positive, if you look for and seek to possess the good that you perceive in situations."[1] He also says, "It takes time and repeated affirmations to change an attitude. However, once you change it, boom, you have let yourself go."[2]

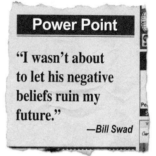

Power Point

"I wasn't about to let his negative beliefs ruin my future."

—*Bill Swad*

Bill succeeded because he was willing to take the risks, had a plan of action, and was determined to overcome obstacles. However, more than anything else, he succeeded because he would not let someone's negative opinion rob him of his positive attitude and expectations.

Power Point Question

Are you letting negative attitudes keep you from pursuing your dreams?

"Choose life, that both you and your descendants may live."
—Deuteronomy 30:19 (NKJV)

News Headline

EXTRA! EXTRA!

Final Edition

Joe Gibbs Rejoins NASCAR

For the second time, Joe Gibbs resigned from coaching the Washington Redskins and returned to NASCAR racing.

Joe Gibbs knows how to make good things happen. The first time he coached the Washington Redskins of the National Football League, the team made the playoffs eight out of twelve seasons. He then retired from football to devote more time to his NASCAR racing team. His NASCAR racing teams have been among the most successful.

Gibbs believes that the ability to create positive motion is one of the keys to effective leadership. Especially when circumstances are negative or lethargic, one should seize it as "an opportunity to lap the field."[1]

Achievers need to have the ability, when the situation demands, to take control, activate the proper actions, break through the barriers of resistance, and embrace opportunities.

MAKING THINGS HAPPEN

I heard a good example of this action-oriented attitude at one of our seminars. It was shared by Jim Money, former head of national employment company Snelling and Snelling Personnel. The story was about Robert Townsend, who was senior vice president of American Express before becoming the highly successful chairman of Avis Rent a Car.

A controller once told Townsend that he thought he could make American Express an extra $800,000 a day. However, he needed a special computer to calculate whether his plan could actually work. Townsend told the controller, "Get one now."

The controller replied, "If I turn in a requisition for one, it will take days, maybe weeks."

"I'll get you one," Townsend answered. He contacted the supply warehouse and found that they had one in stock. However, when he went to obtain it, the supply manager would not release it to him without a formal requisition.

"I've got something better than a requisition," Townsend declared. "Sign this."

"What is it?" the supply manager asked.

"It's my letter of resignation," explained Townsend. "I want you to sign it so that I can deliver this to the president of the company. When I tell him that I am resigning because a senior vice president of American Express can't get a computer from a supplier, he will know who you are."

Power Point

"Seize [negatives] as an opportunity to lap the field."

–Coach Joe Gibbs

He got his computer and the controller used it to make American Express that extra $800,000 a day.

Sometimes, all it takes to cause a breakthrough is someone who will take the initiative and make things happen.

Power Point Question

Have you empowered yourself and your key people to make the decisions necessary to seize opportunities?

"Prepare your minds for action."
—1 Peter 1:13 (NIV)

News Headline

EXTRA! EXTRA!

Final Edition

92-Year-Old Woman Gets 30-Year Mortgage

A bank in Australia has given a 92-year-old woman a 30-year mortgage to buy her first home. The woman became the country's oldest first-time home buyer.

This story is a great example of someone who is looking ahead to the future and activating her dreams. I find forward-thinking mind-sets in the lives of almost all overcomers and great achievers. My friend John Mason shared on the subject of looking ahead at one of my Hawaii Increase Events. John is a best-selling author of several books and gifted teacher.

"Probably the most common strongholds in a person's life are past mistakes and failures. Throughout history great people, at some point in their lives, have failed. Only those who do not try anything, or expect anything, never fail. People who have few failures also have few victories."

DON'T LOSE TOMORROW'S OPPORTUNITIES

John also said, "We must learn to profit from past mistakes, be forward-focused, and invest in the future.

"Whatever stronghold the past may have on us, it can be broken. God does not hold us back. It is our own choosing that keeps us from moving forward. The more we look backward, the less able we are to see forward.

"In Philippians 3:13-14, the apostle Paul wrote, 'This one thing I do, forgetting those things which are behind, and reaching forth unto those things which are before, I press toward the mark for the prize of the high calling.'"

DON'T LOSE TOMORROW'S OPPORTUNITIES

In his book *An Enemy Called Average*, John states, "Here is the key to being free from the stranglehold of past failures, hurts, and mistakes: Learn the lesson but forget the details. Don't roll over and over in your mind the minute details."[1]

My friend Brian Klemmer says, "I have seen thousands of people allow their past to plague their future. Years after a negative event occurred they can't seem to let it go."

John also says, "The past is history. It has no life—unless you continually breathe life into it. Today is the day to begin to shake off those shackles of the past and move forward to your future."

Power Point

"The more we look backward, the less able we are to see forward."
—*John Mason*

Power Point Question

Is some past negative event or memory keeping you from positive opportunities?

"Forgetting those things which are behind, and reaching forth unto those things which are before."
—Philippians 3:13

After the golfer was revived, he said of his friend, "He gave me the gift of life." You also can give the gift of "life" to others—maybe not through CPR, but by speaking positive words into their dreams and self-images.

A teacher released this force into the life of Rich DeVos. DeVos is the cofounder of the world's largest multilevel marketing corporation and is also the owner of the Orlando Magic professional basketball team. At a convention where we both were speaking, he shared about how this power was imparted to him.

ONE OF THE GREATEST GIFTS TO GIVE

DeVos said, "One of the greatest things you can give to another person is the gift of encouragement. It is a gift with starting power and staying power. When I was struggling to find my way as a high school senior, my Bible teacher sent me to a life of significance just by writing a few words in my yearbook: 'With talents for leadership for God's kingdom.' Those words encouraged me to believe that God had a plan for me and my gift.

"That note was written to me more than fifty years ago, but it remains fresh even to this day. With those words echoing in my ears I became determined to make a difference in life."

When I was at dinner with Colin Powell, America's former secretary of state, he shared how he endeavored to be an encourager: "I always show more kindness than appears to be necessary. Most people need this more than you will ever know."[1]

Zig Ziglar concurs saying, "If you can catch people doing something well, no matter how small it may seem, and positively reinforce them for doing it, they will continue to grow in a positive direction."[2]

Richard Branson, who is the founder and president of Virgin Atlantic Airlines and Virgin Records, makes being an encourager is one of his management strategies: "I praise, praise, praise. It brings out the best of people."[3]

Og Mandino said that each of us should, "Extend to each person, no matter how trivial the contact, all the care and kindness and understanding that we can."[4]

Power Point

"Encouragement is a gift with starting power and staying power."

—Rich DeVos

Being an encourager not only helps others, but it can also bless you. According to the late Norman Vincent Peale, "When you encourage others, you fill your own heart with courage."[5]

Determine to be a better encourager by giving to others the "gift of life."

Power Point Question

How often do you publically encourage people?

"Encourage one another daily."
—Hebrews 3:13 (NIV)

News Headline

EXTRA!
EXTRA!

Final
Edition

Man Comes Out Of Coma

A man who had been shot in the head came out of his coma after seven years.

When my son, Rock Harrison, was seven years old, he came out of a coma —not a physical one but rather a "learning coma." At least, that is what it seemed like.

Rock is intelligent and did well in most subjects at school. However, in his younger years, he had great difficulty with reading. He was just not proficient at connecting words in order to make phrases. Because of this deficiency, he was required to repeat first grade.

His reading difficulties continued in second grade. In the early spring of that school year, I was informed by school officials that Rock's reading was still at preschool level. As a result, they planned to make him repeat second grade.

I was distressed. Rock was already the biggest and oldest boy in his class. I felt that holding him back another year could create a self-image problem that could negatively affect him for the rest of his life.

STRATEGIES TO CHANGE SELF-IMAGE

While praying together one night, I felt impressed to develop an action plan consisting of strategies to change my son's self image and help his learning deficiency.

1. PRAISE: I began to praise Rock for the subjects in which he was doing well. I also reminded him of his past and current accomplishments.

2. LOVE: I reaffirmed to him that my love and acceptance of him was not based upon his performance, but rather on his relationship with me.

3. TIME: I rearranged my schedule so that I could give him extra time for reading assistance. I also set aside additional time for playing together and for personal attention.

4. AFFIRMATION: Since beliefs can be changed by repetition, I had him confess the truth of I John 4:4 several times a day: "Greater is he that is in [me], than he that is in the world." In addition, I would continually have him proclaim, "I am a winner!"

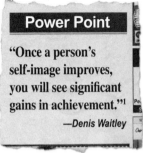

Power Point

"Once a person's self-image improves, you will see significant gains in achievement."[1]

—*Denis Waitley*

ASTONISHING IMPROVEMENT

Soon, I began to see improvement in his ability to read. He got better and better. Still, I was not ready for the great news that would soon come. At a follow-up appointment, school officials proclaimed that they had never seen such rapid improvement as they had with Rock. "In less than ninety days, he has skyrocketed from a preschool reading level to a mid-year third-grade reading level."

Rock not only advanced to the third grade, but on the last day of school he won the award for being the number one reader in his class!

Power Point Question

How can you improve your own or someone else's self-image?

"As a person thinketh in his heart, so is he."
—Proverbs 23:7 (Author's Paraphrase)

News Headline

EXTRA! EXTRA!

Toilet Paper Theft Causes Firing

Police used marked rolls of toilet paper to catch a principal who was stealing from his school.

The markings, which could be seen only under ultraviolet light, proved the official was routinely taking school supplies home.

The principal in the above story had to resign in disgrace. While succeeding in developing his academic credentials, he apparently failed to develop his personal character.

Let's define character. *Merriam-Webster's 11th Collegiate Dictionary* defines *character* as "the complex of mental and ethical traits marking and often individualizing a person, group, or nation." Another definition of character I like is from former congressman J.C. Watts: "Character is doing what is right when no one is looking."[1] My personal definition of character is "the core thinking and values that predetermine a person's behavior."

Character is learned behavior. Good character is best taught at home by precept and example when children are young, as illustrated by the life of my friend Jess Gibson.

A TEST OF CHARACTER

Jess Gibson is an incredible motivational speaker and pastor from Springfield, Missouri. At one of my Increase Events, he shared about a test of character he faced when he was a teenager.

"At the age of 15, I had a before-school job at a local pharmacy. One morning, I was sweeping behind the counter where the cash register was located. All of a sudden, I saw it—a beautiful, crisp $10 bill. It was just lying there on the floor, waiting for me to pick it up. The boss was in the basement. No one else was in the store. Who would know? Should I or shouldn't I take the money?

"I thought about what I could do with ten dollars. Visions of candy and sugar plums danced through my head! Then it dawned on me. At that moment, my trustworthiness, my character, was being tested. How I responded to this temptation would shed light on who I really was and who I would become.

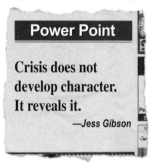

Power Point

Crisis does not develop character. It reveals it.
—*Jess Gibson*

"I picked up the money, ran to the basement, and presented it proudly to the owner. He grumbled that someone had been clumsy handling money. He didn't even say thanks or give me something as a reward.

"However, I received my reward. It was that experience. It revealed to me that I was developing the positive character traits that would help guide me throughout my life and enable me to overcome bigger challenges and temptations."

Each action you take when faced with moral questions or temptations will help form your habits. These habits, in turn, will determine your character.

Power Point Question

How would those close to you describe your character?

———————

"A good name is rather to be chosen than great riches."
—Proverbs 22:1

News Headline

Final Edition

EXTRA!
EXTRA!

Car Falls Seven Floors

A woman's car lurched through a steel barrier and tumbled from the seventh floor of a downtown Pittsburgh parking garage. Miraculously she suffered only minor injuries.

If you ever felt like you were plummeting toward personal or financial destruction or that everything in your life seemed upside down, then Dr. Robert Schuller believes his philosophy of living can help you.

A POSITIVE APPROACH TO LIVING

Dr. Schuller is the author of more than thirty books—five of which have made the *New York Times* best-sellers list. He is also the well-known pastor of the Crystal Cathedral in Garden Grove, California from which he ministers worldwide every week by television.

On several occasions, I have had the opportunity to visit with him, and I have always been impressed with his energy, compassion, and wisdom.

As a young man, while pastoring a small church in Illinois, he somehow got on Dr. Norman Vincent Peale's mailing list. For three years, he received Peale's teachings on positive thinking. He says, "I became internally changed by all of the dozens and dozens of sentences in his sermons. I became a positive thinker."[1]

Dr. Schuller was convinced that he had a powerful message to give, particularly for people who were struggling with adversity in life. In 1955, "with his wife, Arvella, as the organist and $500 in assets, he rented the Orange Drive-in theatre and conducted...services from the roof of the snack bar."[2]

He began to help people by sharing his faith and positive approach to living with those who had never experienced life in that way. The church has continued to until now it has one of the largest congregations in America—plus millions watching weekly on television.

Dr. Schuller says that he became a possibility thinker one day when he was reading his Bible and some words of Jesus leaped off the pages at him: "Nothing will be impossible for you" (Matthew 17:20 NIV). Therefore, all things are possible.

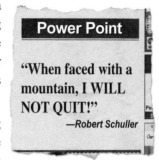

Power Point

"When faced with a mountain, I WILL NOT QUIT!"
—*Robert Schuller*

To Dr. Schuller, possibility thinking is simply "focusing faith on achieving definite goals."[3] This thinking is evidenced in his Possibility Thinker's Creed:

THE POSSIBILITY THINKER'S CREED

When faced with a mountain, I WILL NOT QUIT!

I will keep on striving until

I climb over,

find a pass through, tunnel underneath,

or

simply stay

and

turn the mountain into a gold mine

with God's help![4]

Dr. Schuller believes that really "nobody has a money problem. They only have an idea—a thinking—problem. When you get the right thinking then the ideas and money will be attracted to you."[5]

Power Point Question

How can you better activate possibility-thinking power in your life?

_____

"Nothing will be impossible for you."
—Matthew 17:20 (NIV)

News Headline

Final Edition

EXTRA! EXTRA!

Couple Marries At Airport

A woman surprised her fiancée as he arrived on a flight at the Corpus Christi, Texas airport by greeting him in a wedding gown.

Surrounded by friends and onlookers, a justice of the peace officiated as the couple exchanged wedding vows. After the ceremony, the bride told reporters that the two of them first met in Dallas while each of them were on business trips. Since most of their time had been spend seeing each other in different cities, at airports and on airplanes, it seemed natural to get married in an airport terminal.

My friend, Lynette Lewis, believes in the power of positive surprises. She says, "No matter how hard you work or how dedicated you are, you will find that it is the unplanned surprises that can be the real gifts in life."

Lynette is a corporate marketing expert, author and conference speaker. She has done extensive research on the characteristics of those who achieve continuing success and gain satisfaction at work plus with their personal lives. One of those key characteristics she discovered is the recognition that "the journey will probably be different than what you thought and better than what you imagined."

BE READY FOR THE UNEXPECTED

Lynette instructs achievers to "Be ready for the unexpected. Learn to accept, even embrace, the surprises of life. Constantly be looking for new ways of working with what you have been given and/or possess. Become like an artist. They have a way of taking simple, even ugly, elements and turning them into something of beauty."

In a teaching session at one of my Increase Events she stated, "The block of marble from which Michelangelo carved his famous sculpture of David had already been hacked on by two other artists. Each of them had attempted to carve something from the stone, but in frustration ultimately abandoned the projects. That piece of marble then sat neglected and exposed to the elements for 25 years.

"At the age of 26, unexpectedly Michelangelo was commissioned to finish the work. After three years of labor, he completed a masterpiece that has inspired awe for over 500 years."

Lynette believes that "The key is to recognize that surprises and new opportunities are everywhere. However, many times they are missed because they are buried in situations that appear to be problems or obstacles. They simply require eyes that are willing to see them and a mind that is eager to accept the change."

Power Point

Be ready for the unexpected."

–Lynette Lewis

Former United States Vice President Dick Cheney concurs. While speaking to a graduating class at Louisiana State University he stated, "Many of you will find yourselves following a very different course than you have planned, all because the opportunity came to you out of the blue. Be on the watch for those moments that come along and start you in a new direction."[1]

Learn to live expecting opportunities to be hidden in life's unexpected situations. Your life will take on added excitement and meaning as great surprises and new relationships suddenly appear.

Power Point Question

How well do you respond to the unexpected surprises?

"The steps of a good man are ordered of the Lord."
—Psalm 37:23

"**Y**ou are helping too much if you take responsibility for the care and feeding of other people's monkeys," says Dr. Kenneth Blanchard, coauthor of the *One-Minute Manager.*

In this context, the term "monkey" refers to the tasks, jobs, or problems that are the responsibility of other people, such as subordinates, friends, or children.

When you give in to the temptation to take on problems or jobs that are not yours, in essence, you "put a monkey on your back." This happens when you find yourself saying, "Let me help," or worse yet, "Let me do that for you." The other person may walk away thirty pounds lighter because you just took away his or her monkey. However, you now feel weighed down because the "monkey" is yours to care for.

Blanchard teaches that the two biggest reasons to avoid taking other people's monkeys are: they must be cared for and fed by you; their former owners now check to see how you are doing with their monkeys!

If you put too many of other people's monkeys on your back, it will add stress to your life and reduce the time available for your main responsibilities.

KEEPING THE MONKEYS OFF YOUR BACK

In my Time Increase CD series, I teach three responses that I learned from Blanchard for keeping other people's monkeys off your back.

1. BE UNDERSTANDING: Tell the person that you understand the complexity of the problem and that you feel for him or her. Say that you are willing to talk about how the individual (not you) can get it solved.

2. OFFER SUGGESTIONS: Inform the person that this is his or her responsibility, but also give some suggestions, strategies, and/or ideas to try.

3. GIVE STRATEGIES: If you feel that the other person does not have the ability to handle the monkey, give specific directions. Explain the next move or strategy that you would recommend, and then supervise what the person does.[1]

Power Point

"**Monkeys belong with their rightful owners, not an adoptive parent.**"[2]

—*Dr. Kenneth Blanchard*

By learning how to keep monkeys off your back, you can prevent your life from becoming a zoo!

Power Point Question

What strategies can you use to keep other people's monkeys off your back?

_____

"And Moses' father-in-law said to him, 'The thing that you are doing is not good. You will surely wear out."
—Exodus 18:17-18 (NASB)

I have heard that the practice of watching TV can be a time-waster, but five years? Of course, this man had died. However, many people who are very much alive watch too much TV and/or indulge in activities that have no apparent redemptive value.

An achiever should attempt to eliminate or at least reduce those actions and activities that, in reference to pursuing their dreams and goals, are non-productive.

Dr. Robert Rutherford teaches that "a person cannot effectively deal with wasted or non-productive time until he understands the concept of 'mortgaged time.'" Dr. Rutherford is a popular seminar teacher who specializes in the areas of negotiation and time management. His teaching on mortgaged time has been of great benefit to me.

UNDERSTANDING MORTGAGED TIME

At one of my Increase Events, Dr. Rutherford stated, "There is never enough time to do all the worthwhile and valuable things in life. There is nothing that you can do to get more time. You have exactly 168 hours a week. Since time is precious and irreplaceable, choices must be made. If you promise or commit some of these hours to a person, institution, or task, these hours are now not available for other uses. You have 'mortgaged' your time.

"Your time gets mortgaged because of the commitments you make. These time agreements you make may be visible and may have been done consciously, or they may be more subtle, invisible, and not easily recognized by you. However, whether they are created by conscious decision or by actions and/or habit patterns, they are still real.

"Understanding that you have options as to what you do with your time is the beginning of effective time management. Taking responsibility for these agreements—and considering them in advance of commitments—will enhance your productivity and the quality of your life."

Here are some strategies from Dr. Rutherford that can help you deal with mortgaged time:

1. AWARENESS: Continually be aware of the agreements you are creating that will impact your time and scheduling.

> **Power Point**
>
> **"Time is precious, and...choices must be made."**
> —*Dr. Robert Rutherford*

2. COMMUNICATE: Let others know how you feel about these agreements, and what you believe they are—and are not.

3. DON'T GET STUCK: Sometimes, agreements that worked for you in the past might no longer be supportive of your dreams and goals.

4. RENEGOTIATE: If you are committed to agreements that are no longer productive or meaningful, honor your agreements. At the same time, try to renegotiate or eliminate the ones that are not working.

By activating the above strategies, you can increase productivity while experiencing a more enjoyable and fulfilling life.

Power Point Question

What time/mortgage agreements should you alter or eliminate?

"(Make) the most of your time."
—Ephesians 5:16 (NASB)

News Headline

Final Edition | EXTRA! EXTRA!

Quarterback Leaves Pro Bowl Early

The NFL's starting quarterback left the game - and the stadium - early in order to catch a plane from Hawaii to home.

Even though his playing time had ended, this NFL quarterback stirred up a ruckus when he left for the airport while the game was still in progress. However, he smoothed things over by saying, "I apologize for leaving early, but I just could not wait to get back home to my family and fans."

By describing the reason for his departure in such a masterful manner, this player showed his command of a sales and debate strategy referred to as "reframing." I define reframing as "changing the frame of reference that someone is using to perceive or interpret an experience." The underlying concept is that if you can change people's interpretation or perception, you can change their response and corresponding feelings.

UNDERSTANDING THE REFRAMING TECHNIQUE

Overcoming resistance and gaining understanding using the strategy of reframing can work in both the marketplace and in the personal arena, as evidenced by an experience I had with my oldest daughter, Sandy.

Several years ago, Sandy, who was a teenager at the time, was working in our front yard. Two young men drove up and talked to her from their car. After several minutes, she came up to the house and asked if she could go out with them that night.

Replying that I had never met the boys and knew nothing about them, I suggested that she invite them to our family dinner the following week so all of us could get to know them better.

My response greatly upset Sandy. Her face turned red, and she blurted out, "What wrong, Dad? Don't you trust me?"

Knowing that she was feeling very negative about my answer, I immediately put my reframing mind-set to work. I explained, "Honey, if I had a million dollars in a briefcase, and some stranger came to the house and wanted to borrow it for the evening, would I let him?"

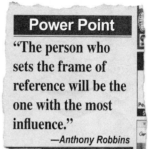

She replied, "Of course not. You would protect it."

"Then you can better understand my response. It is not that I don't trust you. I'm trying to protect you. To me, you—and your reputation—are more valuable than a million dollars in a briefcase."

Immediately, her countenance changed. She became teary eyed as she hugged me saying, "Thank you, Dad, for loving and caring for me so much."

By effectively using the strategy of reframing, I had quickly changed a situation from negative to positive.

Anthony Robbins describes reframing: "In its simplest form, it is the changing of a negative statement into a positive one by changing the frame of reference used to perceive the experience."[1]

If you can change how people think about an event or an occurrence, you can automatically change how they feel about it. That is why you should have the strategy of reframing in your verbal arsenal.

Power Point Question

How can you better use the strategy of reframing?

"You are looking at things as they are outwardly."
—2 Corinthians 10:7 (NASB)

News Headline

With Low-cal Movement, Less Is More

A recent study found that people can significantly reduce their odds of dying of heart disease and extend their longevity by cutting calorie consumption.

Increase—and survival—often go to the sleek and efficient, not the bloated and ponderous. Believing this truth is one of the things that made Robert Crandall so successful. Crandall was chairman of American Airlines from 1982-1998. Under his leadership, American broke out of the pack to become one of the world's largest airlines.

FLYING PLANES THAT ARE TOO BIG

During the time that Crandall was running the airline, he sat across the aisle form me on a flight to Tulsa. We had a wonderful talk about the things I liked and didn't like about American's AAdvantage Frequent Flyer Program and the service of the carrier as a whole.

A few months later, I noticed one of his success strategies at work. At a press conference, he announced that American was disposing of most of its fleet of jumbo jets ad replacing them with smaller jets—Super 80s and 737s. When asked why he was doing this, he replied, "No airline has ever gone broke by flying planes that are too small. Airlines go broke by flying planes that are too big."

With this statement, he released a powerful point to consider. Increase thinkers are prepared to grow and expand as needs demand. However, increase thinking does not always mean that bigger is better. In the case of this airline, it meant something quite different.

American's consumer surveys had revealed to the management that— except on long haul flights—its flyers were more interested in increased frequency of jet departures than in plane size. By flying smaller jets, the airline could offer more flights and at different times. Also, the airline realized that it was much easier to fill smaller jets, resulting in higher load factors and correspondingly greater profits.

I have lost count of the number of times that I have consulted with and prayed for various business leaders and pastors who were in financial difficulty. Analyses of these situations revealed that it was solely because they built facilities that were too big and expensive or because their overhead was too large.

> ## Power Point
>
> **"Dinosaurs became extinct; rabbits still abound."**
>
> *–Laurie Beth Jones*

Jesus taught about this concept. In John 15, he shared how a grapevine's long-term output was actually increased through pruning (cutting back) the branches. Because of this cutting back, the branches could receive more nourishment and strength from the roots. This, in turn, caused more and bigger fruit to be produced.

While you are increase, be careful not to get too big. Also, be ready to temporarily cut back in certain areas if it will result in greater future growth.

As best-selling author Laurie Beth Jones says, "Dinosaurs became extinct; rabbits still abound."[1]

Power Point Question

Are there areas—such as overhead, facilities, staff, debt, or inventory—in which you should reduce costs now in order to increase profits later?

"Every branch that does bear fruit he prunes (trims)
so that it will be even more fruitful."
—John 15:2 (NIV)

There was something very unusual about the opening of this institution of higher learning. This university campus opened without the state putting up any money for land or buildings.

For several years, local officials tried to get the state university system to open a campus in the Coachella Valley area of Southern California, where Palm Desert is located. At the time, residents had to drive over fifty miles if they desired to attend classes at university site. Repeatedly, they were told, "If the state has to pay for it, it will take decades. In fact, it might never happen."

Two local residents would not accept that answer. They teamed up to do something highly unusual. They arranged for the chancellor of the California State University system to come to town for a luncheon with some dignitaries. They also invited several local residents and professional businesspeople. When the chancellor informed them that a new campus was not planned anytime soon, someone asked, "What if we donated a campus to you—lock, stock, and barrel? Then would you open it and furnish the staff?" At first, the chancellor thought it was a joke. No one had ever donated a whole campus before. When he realized that they were serious, he answered, "Yes."

That began the process. They met with city officials, and they agreed to donate a 200-acre site of land for the campus. Then, by combining municipal money with private donations, in ninety days, the two raised $9 million for the first building. While it was being constructed, another $10 million was raised and a second building was completed. Then, the third building was finished.

Now, thousands of students are attending classes. Oh, and the two private citizens are still raising money to keep the construction going.

INTENTION + MECHANISM = RESULTS

These two individuals are using a success formula that I first learned from my friend Brian Klemmer. Brian is a master of group dynamics and a seminar facilitator. At one of my Hawaii Increase Events, he taught about a formula that achievers use to achieve results. The formula is Intention + Mechanism = Results.

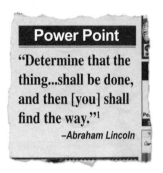

Power Point

"Determine that the thing...shall be done, and then [you] shall find the way."[1]

–Abraham Lincoln

Brian maintains that the key to making things happen is for one to change focus. Instead of concentrating solely on the "how to"(mechanism), put your focus and energies on the hunger/ desire (intention). When someone's intention to do something is strong enough, the various mechanisms will begin to be manifested.

Brian teaches that "one way to raise the intensity of your intention is visualization. To achieve your goal of creating something new, you must surround yourself with pictures of the desired finished state. That will cause your sub-conscious to work on creating mechanisms to raise money to achieve your goal."

Using the above formula can help you to unlock the powerful potential of your subconscious and accomplish what may seem impossible or insurmountable.

Power Point Question

What can you do visually to increase your intention?

"Write the vision, and make it plain."
—Habakkuk 2:2

Power Point #37

News Headline — Final Edition — EXTRA! EXTRA!

Bugging Devices Cause Political Furor

Listening devices were found in the offices of the mayor of Philadelphia. The FBI acknowledged that they were responsible for planting the bugs.

A political furor erupted, following the disclosure that a Democrat, who was in a bitter election battle with a Republican, had his offices bugged by a department of the federal government that is headed by a Republican. The FBI stated that the bugs were placed as part of a criminal investigation and were not political espionage. However, many were not sure that was the case.

If the thought of federal officials "bugging" the offices of an elected official alarms you, consider this story: Some time ago, one foreign country's security intelligence agency warned its top businesspeople not to fly a certain European air carrier. The reason: They discovered that the airline's first- and business-class sections had bugs—electronic bugs. Not only that, but it was also reported that the airline had undercover agents who were posing as flight attendants in order to steal corporate secrets from the unsuspecting business travelers who were on their planes.[1]

In another case of possible bugging, "A recent court case revealed that the FBI had used the popular OnStar [information and emergency assistance] system [that comes on many new cars] to...monitor private conversations."[2] Unknown to most people, within the OnStar system is a passive listening feature which gives it the potential to eavesdrop on unsuspecting motorists.[3]

Also consider the fact that many cell phones on the market come with internal cameras. This technology enables someone to discreetly and quickly record anything from unpublished financial data to a CEO's faux pas at the company holiday party. Those images can be transmitted via e-mail to a competitor or media outlet in a matter of seconds.[4]

Power Points for Increase

Or even closer to home, the last time you signed on to the Internet, it is possible that someone could have intercepted your signal and recorded what you wrote or bought and then shared that information with various marketers, other curious parties, or even the news media.

SAFEGUARDING CONFIDENTIAL INFORMATION

The point of all these stories is this: The more successful you become, the more vulnerable you are to bugging. Therefore, it is imperative that you give greater importance to protecting the confidentiality of your conversations and documents.

Power Point

"Protection is not a principle, but an expedient.""

–Benjamin Disraeli

If you don't implement safeguards, then private information may become available to competitors, dishonest or superambitious employees, or anyone who might steal your briefcase, snatch your laptop computer, or visit your office after hours.

Conduct a security vulnerability inspection. Develop systems and policies that will minimize your risk of unintended information distribution, corporate piracy, or identity theft.

A "bug problem" could cause more than a political furor; it could cost you your reputation and/or business.

Power Point Question

Do you or your company have a security awareness problem?

"Discretion will protect you, and understanding will guard
you."
—Proverbs 2:11 (NIV)

Final Edition **News Headline** EXTRA! EXTRA!

Parents Made Kids Eat Rats And Roaches

Chicago police arrested the parents of four children who had been abused and fed boiled rats and deep-fried roaches.

The average person is appalled to read about such abuse by parents. Yet I wonder how many parents feed their children verbal rats and roaches.

Many psychologists believe that if children (or spouses or employees) are continuously yelled at and told that they are dumb, clumsy, unattractive, or can't do anything right, negative self-images will be formed in their minds.

SELF-IMAGE REPRODUCES ITSELF

Robert Schuller said, "The need for dignity, self-worth, self-respect, and self-esteem are the deepest of all human needs. Unsatisfied, it will result in boredom, restlessness, and is the dawn to dangerous adventures. Unsatisfied, it will drive one to destructive actions and dishonest manipulations. A person's self-image will always reproduce itself in action."[1]

Zig Ziglar affirmed this belief, stating, "A person cannot perform as a winner if he does not see himself as a winner."[2]

Some time ago, I heard a story that came from Greek mythology that illustrates this point. Pygmalion was a king who sculpted a beautiful statue of a lady out of ivory. He then fell in love with it. Aphrodite, the Goddess of Love, shot an arrow into the statue's heart, and it came to life.

From this story comes what is referred to as the Pygmalion Theory: This theory states, "People will become like the image that is conveyed to them."

Probably more than anything else, the words of others form and shape an individual's self-image. Just as one's diet of food can make one physically well or sick, the diet of words that one receive can make one mentally or emotionally well or sick.

Therefore, each of us needs to be aware that the opinions that we give and the words that we speak to others will add to or take away from their self-images. Again, this is a key reason why Colin Powell makes it a practice to speak positive words to people. He told me, as I wrote earlier, "I always try to show more kindness to people that appears to be necessary. Most people need this more than you will ever know."[3]

Power Point

"People will become like the image that is conveyed to them."

–Pygmalion Theory

JAWS OF LIFE

Fire departments in many cities possess a mechanical device called the Jaws of Life. This tool can cut through doors or twisted wreckage in order to free trapped victims. Your mouth is like that tool. It can be a powerful force of hope and encouragement, freeing victims trapped by negative circumstances and poor self-images. Determine today that you are going to be a person who has the "jaws of life."

Power Point Question

Do you consistently try to build up others?

"A word fitly spoken is like apples of gold in settings of silver."
—Proverbs 25:11 (NKJV)

W hen Andre—the man in the above story—decided with his friends to rob someone at an ATM, it seemed like a good idea. Yet all he got was $43, a few credit cards and a prison term.

However, a football coach gave him a second chance and now he has a dream for a new future. He is graduating from college and plans on becoming a coach, saying, "That man gave me a new lease on life."

Sometimes, all someone needs is a fresh opportunity. This is true not only for those who have made wrong decisions, but also for those who have had a loss.

My mother, who passed away in 2003 at the age of ninety-one, was such a person. She experienced the sudden and untimely death of my father when she was only sixty. When Dad died, it was as if her joy and purpose for living left also. She said, "In losing my husband, I felt like Job of old: I had lost everything."

A NEW LEASE ON LIFE

Mom worked her way out of her season of despair. She decided to help others who had lost a loved one through death, separation, or divorce. She began conducting monthly meetings at her home for hurting people. They would gather together for a time of sharing and prayer. Her gatherings were called "New Lease on Life."

Because of the success of these meetings, her home gatherings expanded to other cities. Eventually, they became an organization with chapters across America.

In her book, *A Second Chance at Love*, Mom shared the inspiration that led her out of her despair: "In contrast to the philosophy of God helping those who help themselves, I found that oftentimes He helps those who can't help themselves. God meets us at our point of weakness."[1]

"Trying to recover in our own strength leads to weariness and failure. As long as I focused on the 'I' rather than the 'I Am,' I was disillusioned... It took a complete surrender to God for me to find peace with myself.

Power Point

"God meets us at our point of weakness."

–Edna Harrison-Harlin

"That was my turning point. Once I allowed Him to begin the resurrection in my life, God began to work in ways that were beyond my wildest dreams. He showed me that helping others would also help me. It is a strange but proven biblical principle, 'Give and you shall receive.'"

Mom did receive satisfaction and joy from helping others. She also received something else. A retired rear admiral, who was a widower, came to one of the meetings. They started dating and shortly thereafter became happy newlyweds. Soon, they were traveling together across the globe.

My mother's life changed for the better when she put her focus on others. So will yours.

Power Point Question

List three things that you can do this month to help those who are hurting.

"Satisfy the needs of the oppressed, then your light
will rise in the darkness."
—Isaiah 58:10 (NIV)

News Headline

Man Hugs Tree To Escape Fine

A New York City deli owner was given a $1000 fine because he chained his bicycle to a tree in front of his store.

Commissioners stated that the man was guilty of "tree abuse." However, they agreed to forgive the fine if the owner consented not to abuse the tree again. In addition, the man was required to hug the tree for news photographers.

Hugs might not greatly affect trees, but there is growing evidence that people respond favorably touch and hugs.

My friend Dewey Freidel, who is a seminar speaker and motivational coach for pro athlete teams, actually teaches on the benefits of hugging.

Dewey states, "Something as simple as a hug or touch can make a big difference in someone's life. Many people spend time stroking their cats or dogs. Meanwhile, their spouses and children are across the room literally starving for their affection or a touch."[1]

A meaningful touch is a "gentle pat, a stroke, or a hug given to or received from a significant person."

HOW IMPORTANT IS A HUG OR TOUCH?

In a study conducted by Purdue University, the researchers asked librarians, as students were handed their library cards, to "accidentally" touch every other student. Afterward, the students were interviewed. All the students who had been touched as they were handed their cards gave researchers favorable comments about the library and the librarian.[2]

In another study, Dr. Dolores Krieger, a professor of nursing at New York University, conducted research proving that there is a physiological benefit to touching one another. The study showed that when a person receives a positive touch, that person's hemoglobin levels instantly rise. Hemoglobin is the pigment in red blood cells that carries oxygen to the body. As a result of touch, oxygen is released in great proportions into the blood stream, causing energy to be immediately released. Touch was also shown to help people recover from sickness quicker.[3]

Hugging has been even shown to improve marriages. Laurence Roy Stains and Stephen Bechtal did a national survey of 2,102 women for their book *What Women Want*. In the study, the women reported that when their husbands took time to hug and kiss them, other than when they were in the bedroom expecting sex, they felt that they were respected and adored for their own sake.[4]

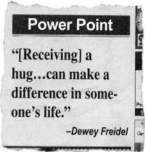

> **Power Point**
>
> **"[Receiving] a hug...can make a difference in someone's life."**
>
> *–Dewey Freidel*

However, there is one caution. According to best-selling author Mark Victor Hansen, "In our culture physical contact between two people who barely know each other might be considered taboo. However, done correctly, a hug is a perfect way of immediately giving and receiving love from another human being."[5]

Be sure to use wisdom as to the appropriateness of the gesture. However, making meaningful touches and proper hugging a part of your daily routine can give others an emotional boost.

Power Point Question

How many positive touches and hugs are you giving out a day?

_____

"People were bringing little children to Jesus to have him
touch them."
— Mark 10:13 (NIV)

News Headline

Final Edition

EXTRA! EXTRA!

Amateur Golfer Shoots 59

The golfer described his feelings as "surreal" and "in disbelief" after he shot a record-breaking 59 on a par-72 golf course at a resort in California.

The man in the above story inspires people to achieve greater success in golf. My friend Peter Lowe inspires people to achieve greater success in life.

Peter's success seminars attract audiences of 20,000, 30,000, and more. He has been featured in *Time, USA Today, Selling,* and *People* magazines and on CNN.

In 1981, Peter heard me speak at a meeting in Vancouver, Canada. At the time, he was selling microcomputers and calculators to businesses. Although he enjoyed sales, he was not fulfilled. He thought, "If I became the greatest salesman in Canada, it would not make me happy."

Peter wanted his life to have an impact on the lives of others. He made the decision to become a sales trainer and motivator of people.

When he conducted his first seminar, he had an audience of 4 people (including his mother). During his early years of speaking, Peter had to memorize his presentations word for word. But he was diligent, faithful, and committed. Even in the face of unbelievable obstacles and intense competition, his meetings got bigger and bigger. In just ten years, he went from starting his business to becoming the most popular conductor of success seminars in the world, drawing the largest audiences.

From my notes of our times together, here are some of his success strategies.

PETER LOWE'S SUCCESS STRATEGIES

1. PERSEVERE: "A person cannot become really successful in anything until he or she determines not to quit."

2. BE DILIGENT: "Watch the details. I personally analyze at least thirty pages of computer reports every day in order to maximize attendance and income."

3. SUSTAIN PROPER INPUT: "Keep yourself on a consistent and regular feeding program of books, tapes, and seminars. Fellowship with other achievers."

Power Point

"Most achievers do not feed themselves enough."

–Peter Lowe

4. THINK PIGGYBACK: "We increased our revenues greatly by offering program options, such as a VIP seating section and idea-exchanging lunches."

5. BE AWARE OF TIMING: "There is a right time to change things. Often, the timing of something is as important as what is done."

6. BE CONSISTENT: "You may change your tactics and methods, but stay with your core principles and calling."

7. LEARN FROM OTHERS: "A wise person learns from his mistakes. A wiser person learns from the mistakes of others."

8. PLAN LONG TERM: "Success takes time. I am much more interested in where I will be in five years than I am in the next seminar."

I got insight into another one of Peter's success strategies when I asked him, "How did you come to be the person who is putting on the largest success seminars in the world?" He replied, "I put on the best small seminars in the world."

Power Point Question

What are you doing to rise to a higher level of success?

———————————

"Wise men lay up knowledge."
—Proverbs 10:14

News Headline EXTRA! EXTRA!

Final Edition

Survivors Gather At Reunion

Many of the crew and passengers who were onboard U.S. Airways Flight #1549 celebrated still being alive. The passenger jet that they were on hit a flock of birds that knocked out both of its engines.

With no power, the pilot, Captain Chesley 'Sully' Sullenberger, was able to glide the plane to a safe landing on New York's Hudson River. Since then he has appeared on numerous national television programs, been hosted at the White House, was Grand Marshal of America's largest parade—The Tournament of Roses, plus, wrote a book.

Over the ensuing months that followed this incident, I read several stories written about how this amazing pilot responded to the crisis. As I did, I realized that some of the strategies he used were the same as those that an effective leader should use if and when unexpected misfortune confronts them.

HOW TO RESPOND TO UNEXPECTED "BIRD STRIKES"

1. TAKE CONTROL: The co-pilot was actually in control of the aircraft when the bird collision occurred. Immediately, Captain Sullenberger exclaimed, "I'll take it."

As a leader, in times of crisis you must immediately reorganize your priorities and put the total focus upon analyzing and re-stabilizing the situation at hand. In most crisis situations, more than anything else, what is done right at the beginning will determine the eventual outcome.

2. SEEK ADVICE – BUT YOU DECIDE: Air traffic controllers on the ground advised the crew to turn the plane around and return to New York's LaGuardia Airport. Captain Sullenberger listened to their reasoning but then declared, "No, we are going to land in the Hudson."

In the same manner, an effective leader should seek the wise counsel of advisors, counselors, accountants, lawyers, etc. However, you cannot let them be the decision makers. You are the only one who really knows the situation at hand, plus only you have the knowledge and experience to determine what the best response is in order to handle the unfolding crisis.

Power Point

"My whole life had been a preparation for that moment."[1]

–Captain 'Sully' Sullenberger

3. ESTIMATE YOUR HOLDING POWER: There was a reason that Captain Sullenberger choose to land the plane in the river. Being a glider pilot, he knew that if the jet was flying at an elevation of 3,000 feet he could only glide the plane about three miles (1,000 feet of descent per mile.) Therefore, when traffic controllers suggest that he return to his originating airport, he knew that it was over three miles away and the distance was too great.

If you suddenly lose your financial, physical or emotional thrust, you must quickly determine your "gliding range." By that I mean, How far and how long can you or your business stay airborne—financially, physically and emotionally? Also, you must assess if there is anything that you can do to increase that time frame.

4. EXPECT GOD TO INTERVENE: The picture of the passengers standing upon the wing of the plane after its impact on the river is a scene that I will never forget. Not only would this plane not fall from the sky, but when in the water, it would not sink.

Know that in spite of how negative the situation might appear, God's power can quickly change circumstances. Have confidence that the God who began a good work can guide and empower you to overcome adversity and to complete the task that He has called you to do.

Power Point Question

How effectively can you handle an unexpected "bird strike?"

"Under (or upon) His wings, I will find refuge."
—Psalm 91:4

Several days of torrential rains had collapsed a century-old sewer. Over time, the water washed away the earth beneath the home's foundation, causing the collapse.

Across the globe, many other homes are falling into sinkholes. However, these sinkholes are emotional and are caused by collapsing marriages and shattered dreams.

Like the home in the above story, many of these relationships appeared to be resting on solid ground. Then, suddenly, everything gave way. This happened because, underneath the exterior trappings, over time, the very foundations of these relationships had eroded and washed away. Couples and entire families then suffered because of hurts, separation, and emotional trauma.

Several factors can cause a relationship to collapse. It might be the result of a lifestyle of continuous stress, which attacks a couple's intimacy and communication. Maybe it is wrong priorities brought on by self-absorption or the accumulation of material things. Perhaps it comes from continued verbal abuse. Or it could be the boredom that sets in when old dreams and goals are attained and new ones are not created.

How can you reinforce the foundation of your significant relationship and help prevent a sinkhole? Here are some strategies that I have learned my own experiences and from interviewing couples who are experiencing long-term loving relationships.

RELATIONSHIP REINFORCEMENT STRATEGIES

1. COMMUNICATION: Learn to listen carefully, not just to the words being expressed, but also to the feelings behind the words.

2. AWARENESS: Become more aware of each other's needs and desires.

3. PLAYING TOGETHER: Have fun and share pleasurable times with each other. Schedule activities that both of you enjoy.

4. ESCAPE: Periodically, break your normal schedules and routines of life. Take trips together to dream spots. Disappear for a long lunch or a weekend away together.

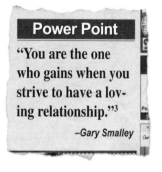

Power Point

"You are the one who gains when you strive to have a loving relationship."[3]

–Gary Smalley

5. PRAISE: Nourish each other's egos and self-image through positive affirmations and sincere praise.

6. ROMANCE: Never stop dating. Practice being kind and caring to one another. Schedule quiet times for just the two of you.

7. WORSHIP: Share common spiritual experiences. This will add depth, power, and intimacy to your relationship.

If you are not already doing so, activate these strategies. They will work when applied over a period of time with persistence and a loving attitude. You may not only avoid the sudden collapse of an important relationship, but you will also experience a life that is more exciting and fulfilling.

Best-selling author Gary Smalley states, "You may feel that it is impossible to change lifelong habits, but it is not. So try to change yours. As you make progress, you will gain confidence."[1] He continues, "But, don't expect miracles overnight. Anything of genuine worth takes time to perfect. As time passes, you will find yourself succeeding more frequently. Soon you will be right in the midst of the kind of marriage you never thought possible."[2]

Power Point Question

What can you do to the foundation of your loving relationship?

———————

"The wise [person] builds [his or her] house."
—Proverbs 14:1 (NASB)

When Danny Cahill weighed in at 430 pounds, virtually no one thought that in a little over six months, he could lose 239 pounds. But he did. His reward? Over $1,000 for every pound that he lost.

As I watched on television the celebration of Danny winning the contest, I thought about the enormous price that he had to pay to achieve that victory: the strict diet that he placed himself on, the hours and hours in the gym lifting weights plus doing numerous exercises and running for uncountable miles on a treadmill. In addition, he had a season of absence from normal social activities and all of this taking place while he was separated from his family.

Therein lies an irony of life. I have discovered that...

MANY WANT THE REWARDS.
FEW ARE WILLING TO PAY THE PRICE.

Thinking about having a willingness to pay the price reminds me of a story shared by Gary Richardson at one of my Increase Events.

Gary is one of Oklahoma's top attorneys. He has received numerous awards and distinctions including one for winning a state record lawsuit settlement. One day Gary received a call from his son, Chuck, who was attending university. Chuck told Gary that he planned to drop a math course before a big exam the following week because the course was too difficult.

That night, Gary met with his son and told him that he wasn't being honest with himself about what the issue really was. He stated, "You may have to study 30, 50, or 70 hours this weekend to do well on the exam. But you are smart, and if you put in the study time, you can pass. The issue is not your ability, it is simply, are you willing to pay the price?"[2]

Gary continued, "There is another thing to consider. Throughout your life you'll be faced with difficult challenges. How you react to each of these occasions will develop a habit pattern. Either you respond with, 'I will cut and run' or 'I will meet the challenge.' The decision about this course could be the beginning of you developing one of these patterns. Which pattern do you desire for your life?"

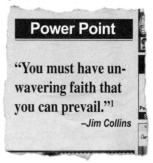

Power Point

"You must have unwavering faith that you can prevail."[1]

–Jim Collins

Chuck decided to stay in the math course and he spent the entire weekend studying. The following Tuesday he took the exam, and made the top grade in the class. Not only that, he began to develop a habit pattern of overcoming difficult situations. After graduation, he started practicing law with his father and went on to become the country's district attorney.

Both Chuck and Danny decided to pay the price of change. As a result their lives have gone from normal to significant. When facing a challenge, or in reacting to adversity, how you respond helps to form your habit patterns which in turn will determine your destiny.

Power Point Question

Are you willing to pay the price?

"We are well able to overcome."
—Numbers 13:30

News Headline — EXTRA! EXTRA!
Final Edition

New York Cabbie's Check Bounces

A New York cabbie took a man all the way from New York to Michigan and back and received a bad check.

After the 3-day, 32-hour trip, the taxi driver got a $2000 check for the fare. Police reported that the check was no good and that the cab driver was sick in bed.

One does not need to be a cab driver to be "taken for a ride." I could not begin to count all of the counseling calls, e-mails and prayer requests that I have received from salespeople and business owners who were having financial difficulties because of slow-paying or uncollectible accounts.

In most instances, I discovered that many of these people regularly provide goods and/or services to customers based solely upon a purchase order number, a verbal order, or a customer's promise to pay. Then, if the client failed to pay, they have to eat their losses. Not only that, but they also lost the profits they would have made by selling to someone else.

If you want to avoid this kind of scenario from happening to you, here are some helpful loss-prevention strategies.

LOSS-PREVENTION STRATEGIES

1. REDUCE YOUR EXPOSURE: On large projects or orders, require payment as the job progresses. Maybe collect one-third at inception, one-third at midpoint, and one-third at completion. If things go bad, having such a policy will greatly reduce your losses.

2. ESTABLISH CREDIT LIMITS: If you must extend credit, have predetermined, written policies regarding how much credit you are willing to extend. These policies could be based upon a customer's credit history, collateral, or the relationship you have with the client.

3. ELIMINATE ACCOUNTS RECEIVABLE: When possible, eliminate the risks by not having accounts receivable. Instead, accept credit or debit cards, subscribe to a check guarantee system, offer bank financing, or just say, "Cash only."

4. PRE-CHECK CREDIT: If you are going to extend credit, have some method of checking the person or company's credit in advance. Schedule times to periodically review credit.

Power Point

Prevention is better than cure.[1]

–Erasmus

5. INSPECT ACCOUNTS REGULARLY: Also, if you do carry accounts or extend credit, have a system in place for regular billing and follow-up procedures. Review these accounts at regular intervals.

6. PRAY ABOUT YOUR ACCOUNTS: Throughout its pages, the Bible gives examples of times where God gave understanding, wisdom, warning, and favor in the affairs of men.

Instituting the above policies will allow you to spend more of your time making money, not trying to collect it. Remember, what is important is not what you bill, but rather what you actually collect.

Power Point Question

How can you better avoid and handle unexpected collection losses?

"Be thou diligent to know the state of thy flocks."
—Proverbs 27:23

Power Point #46

News Headline

Cruise Ship Runs Aground

A sternwheeler passenger ship developed steering problems while cruising about 80 miles upriver from Portland, Oregon, and ran aground.

Gavin and Patti MacLeod's ship also ran aground. Only it was their personal "love boat" that crashed on the rocks of divorce.

Gavin, who is a celebrated actor, has played leading roles on television series. He is probably best known for his role as the captain of *The Love Boat*. He met Patti while taking tap-dancing lessons in a class she was teaching. Gavin says, "I loved Patti from the time we first met."[1]

After they were married, Gavin's demanding schedule and weeks away from home took a toll. One day, he sent her a letter and asked for a divorce.

Patti says, "The experience of divorce was worse than anything I had ever been through. It was worse than my father leaving the family when I was a little girl, worse than my mother's death. I felt pain twenty-four hours a day."[2]

Finding herself hurt and in confusion, she started seeing therapists. They advised her to forget Gavin and get on with her life. On the other hand, some of her close friends kept telling her that, if she still loved Gavin, she should "hang on" and that "God is a God of restoration."

Choosing to believe that God would heal their broken relationship, she began to earnestly pray for herself, her husband, and their marriage.

Not long afterward, Gavin unexpectedly called and asked her to attend a social event. She suggested that, instead of going out, maybe he would like to come over to her home for dinner.

When Gavin arrived and stood in the doorway, Patti greeted him with her now-classic line, "Your dinner is a little cold. It's been waiting three years."

The couple began dating again. Soon thereafter they were remarried. Every time that I am with them, either socially or at a television studio, they radiate joy, happiness, love, and energy. Now, by sharing their experience in meetings and on television, they bring hope, joy, and laughter to others around the world.

From our times together, here are some of Patti and Gavin's marriage success strategies.

PATTI AND GAVIN'S MARRIAGE SUCCESS STRATEGIES

1. CELEBRATE TOGETHERNESS: Embrace activities as a team. Go places together, meet friends together, and make decisions together.

2. GIVE EACH OTHER SPACE: Don't try to possess or control all the other person's time or activities. Set aside time for each of you to do the activities you individually enjoy.

3. BE CARING: Friends do not deliberately hurt each other. They talk things out. Demonstrate by your words and actions that your partner's wants and needs are important.

4. PRAY TOGETHER: Everything that happens in a day can be influenced by those precious moments spent together in the presence of God.

According to Patti, by making these strategies the foundation of their relationship, they are more in love than ever before.

Power Point Question

How many of the above strategies are you actively using in your marriage?

_____

"[The husband] must love his wife as he loves himself,
and the wife must respect her husband."
—Ephesians 5:33 (NIV)

News Headline

Final Edition

EXTRA! EXTRA!

City Starts Automated Trash Removal

Honolulu's new refuse service features trucks equipped with mechanical arms. The driver collects and dumps trash from standard-sized, city-supplied 96-gallon trash bins. This process makes it quicker and easier to collect trash.

The city of Honolulu has developed a process that makes it quicker and easier to get rid of trash. Paper pile-up can be a big problem, not only with cities, but also with individuals.

Being surrounded by piles of paper can cause stress that smothers creativity and brings feelings of anxiety and loss of control. An achiever can use up so much energy dealing with an influx of mail, memos, and periodicals that he or she loses valuable time—time that could be better spent nurturing and training people and/or doing other important tasks.

Success guru Peter Drucker teaches, "All work takes place in time and uses up time. Yet most people take time for granted. Nothing else, perhaps, distinguishes effective executives as much as their tender loving care of time."[1]

Professional organizers say that the key to increasing productivity by eliminating paper messes is to develop a personalized system—one that works and makes sense for the individual. The main concept behind any paper reduction system is based upon giving priorities to incoming paper flow.

Motivational speaker Patrick Morley teaches that priorities "are pre-decisions that we make in advance that decide what we give our time and attention to. Priorities become the grid that helps us to distinguish opportunity from distraction."[2]

My friend Al Andrews, who is the former chief financial officer of Lockheed Aircraft, believes that "without a well-thought-out plan to direct you specifically, you will get off course."[3]

The key strategy behind any effective program is this: Avoid stacking incoming papers in a pile to be dealt with later. Everything needs to have a place, wherever that may be.

Here are some effective systems for paper reduction.

PAPER REDUCTION SYSTEMS

1. ACT ON IT: Create a "hot folder" for urgent matters. If something is important and you must personally take care of it, get it done as quickly as possible.

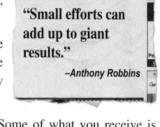

2. REFER IT TO SOMEONE: If it is important but can be handled by someone else, forward it to that person.

3. SAVE IT/FILE IT: Some items must be referred to in the future. Develop an easy-to-use retrieval system to help locate documents quickly when needed.

4. THROW IT AWAY—REDUCE IT: Some of what you receive is not applicable or important. Open your mail standing next to a trash container. Better yet, have subordinates sift through the mail and forward only important items and articles to you.

5. HALT IT: The less you receive, the less you have to deal with. Cancel subscriptions that are not beneficial.

Activating these strategies can free you for new levels of creativity and productivity while increasing your desktop space. As Anthony Robbins teaches, "Small efforts can add up to giant results."[4]

Power Point Question

What systems can you create for better paper-flow management and elimination?

"Let all things be done decently and in order."
—1 Corinthians 14:40

Billy Graham has been called "the national's premier revivalist." Graham has filled sports stadiums around the world with the simple message that people need spiritual fulfillment in their lives. For over fifty years, this influential figure's words have reached television audiences, churchgoers, and U.S. presidents. He has been featured more than thirty times on the Gallup Poll's annual "World's Most Admired Men" list.

For a number of years, Graham has had Parkinson's disease. This condition has made it impossible for him to drive a car or write by hand, but he is making the most of his days. He is still conducting crusades and appearing on television. An estimated 2.5 billion people around the world tuned in to watch the Billy Graham television special, *Starting Over.*

I was privileged to be at the special banquet honoring Graham with the Congressional Medal. The ceremony was attended by members of the house and senate, as well as Bill Clinton, who was then president of the United States. The award was given for "outstanding and lasting contributions to morality, racial equality, family, philanthropy, and religion."[1]

At the banquet, President Clinton stated, "Billy Graham has touched hundreds of millions of lives. He has helped many people in positions of power and influence keep, or regain, their bearings. To me, he is a model of Christian charity."

Former president George H. W. Bush has shared that Graham was also a great help to him: "I cannot tell you what Billy Graham's presence, and his faith, meant to me as president and commander-in-chief. His beliefs and faith gave me great strength."[2]

SUCCESS SECRET: A GOOD CHARACTER AND REPUTATION

One of Graham's secrets of success is his reputation for integrity and right living. His commitment to living a life of character has given his ministry longevity.

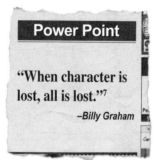

Power Point

"When character is lost, all is lost."[7]

–Billy Graham

For example, in 1948, while conducting meetings in California, he and his staff created and agreed to abide by what they called the "Modesto Manifesto." Graham described the agreement as a "shared commitment" to integrity and purity in which they would, among other things, avoid "financial abuses" and "any situation that would have even the appearance of compromise or suspicion."[3] From that time, Graham did not "travel, meet, or eat alone with a woman other than (his) wife."[4]

My friend Edwin Cole, who had a great ministry to men and authored over fifteen books before his death, stated, "Character is not the same as personality. Personality is seen in public; character is built by what you do in private. There are 'has-beens' in every area of life—music, movies, television, sports, and ministry. Many of these people built their personalities, but neglected their character. When a person's personality wears off, only their character remains."[5]

Make having a good reputation a foundational part of your life. In the words of the late College Basketball Hall of Fame Coach John Wooden, "Ability and talent may get you to the top. It takes character to keep you there."[6]

Power Point Question

How can you increase the power of your reputation?

———————

"Create in me a clean heart."
—Psalm 51:10

News Headline

Final Edition

EXTRA! EXTRA!

Asian Elephant Born In Captivity

Riccardo has become the first second-generation Asian elephant ever to be born in captivity.

Riccardo was born at the Center for Elephant Conservation, a private 200-acre facility operated by the Ringling Bros. and Barnum & Bailey Circus. Since 1992, the circus' breeding program has had 16 elephant births, including Riccardo's parents. Because of the scarcity of Asian elephants, Ringling Bros. is breeding its own elephants, many of which will eventually perform in the circus. In this way, the circus is planning ahead to secure a key element of its future. Ringling Bros. recognizes that, in order to ensure continued success, they must make plans for the future.

My friend Myles Munroe believes that "there is no future without planning."[1] Myles is an international motivational speaker, best-selling author, lecturer, and consultant for governments and businesses. He teaches leaders how to maximize their potential.

He says, "Most people try to live their lives without any real thought of planning. They are like a contractor trying to construct a building without a blueprint. As a result, their lives are out of balance and unreliable…plus they end up unsatisfied and frustrated."[2]

Myles states, "I am a stickler for planning. Anyone who works for me will tell you that I have plans for next week, next year, and five years from now."[3]

One of the key strategies used by Lee Iacocca, former president of Chrysler Corporation, was planning ahead. At a time when Chrysler was in the midst of astronomical cash shortages, asset liquidation, massive layoffs, and possible bankruptcy, Iacocca set aside $750 million to launch a new product—the Caravan. A reporter asked him why he did it. Iacocca replied, "I had to. If you eat the seed corn, you have no future."[4]

Microsoft founder Bill Gates believes that this strategy is one of their company's keys to success. He states, "The key trade-off is how much money to put into present consumption versus how much you put into future products and improvement."[5]

MAKE INVESTMENTS IN YOUR FUTURE

In the personal arena, as well, those who are wise plan and make investments in their future. Instead of spending all their income, they choose to set aside a certain amount for their future needs and retirement.

Planning and budgeting for the future does not come naturally in our "I want mine now" society. The key is this: Make delayed gratification a part of thinking and planning. Otherwise, you will find yourself fighting recurring battles with debt, relationship problems, health difficulties, and shortages.

Power Point

"There is no future without planning."

–*Myles Munroe*

If you desire to live a lifestyle of increase now and in the future, then determine to set aside—regardless of circumstances—a certain amount of your present time, energy, and money as "seed" for future harvests.

Power Point Question

Do you need to be better focused on planning for the future?

<hr>

"Consider (the ant's) ways and be wise!...it stores its provisions
in summer and gathers its food at harvest."
—Proverbs 6:6, 8 (NIV)

As the tornado shattered the woman's house, the fierce winds blew the tub into the woods. When the storm had subsided, the woman crawled out of the tub, suffering only some bruises and scratches during her ordeal.

One evening, my friend Sue Boss experienced a different kind of storm. Rather than destroying her home, it ripped through her heart and shattered her life.

A group of people from the church she attended was returning from seeing a passion play in Eureka Springs, Arkansas. Her son was on his motorcycle. Following him was her husband, who was riding with the church's pastor on his bike.

Apparently, her son, who had been up studying all night the night before, fell asleep. His cycle crossed the centerline and hit an 18-wheeler truck head-on. The impact with the truck killed the boy instantly. The collision also damaged the front axle of the semi, causing the driver to lose control of his rig. The truck then crossed the centerline. It struck the second bike, killing her pastor and her husband.

Sue says, "I was just numb. Most of my family was gone—in one day. Not only did I have to suffer from this devastating loss, but I had to deal with other issues. I didn't know if we had $10 or $10,000 in the bank, or if we even had life insurance. Also, there was a good possibility the trucking company was going to sue me."

Through all that she faced, Sue's faith in God undergirded her in her season of grief. It gave her comfort and hope for the future.

Sue became very active in a local church, volunteering to help others in need. This giving of herself helped her to work through her grief. It also provided the venue where, sometime later, she met a sharp businessman who was a widower. After a season of courtship, they were married.

Today, the couple serves as pastors of a thriving church in Austin, Texas. The church has a strong community outreach and buses hundred of kids to special monthly youth events.

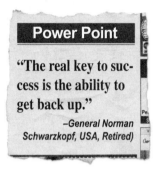

When I was at dinner with General Norman Schwarzkopf, he made a powerful statement about handling negative events: "In life, there will be setbacks. The real key to success is the ability to get back up."

Former Dallas Cowboys coach Tom Landry shared the same viewpoint, stating, "More than anything else, your reaction to adversity will determine your success or failure."[1]

What transpired in Sue Boss's life demonstrates a great truth. Even after it appears that dreams have been destroyed, one can experience a beautiful future.

Power Point Question

Has a negative experience or loss been holding you back?

_____

"Though I walk through the valley of the shadow of death,
I will fear no evil: for thou art with me."
—Psalm 23:4

If one gets on the wrong flight they will end up in the wrong city. Steven Covey, author of several *New York Times* best-selling books including *Seven Habits of Highly Effective People*, believes that is a problem many people face as it relates to life: They are in motion but unsure of where they are going. He says, "If you want to have a successful enterprise [or trip], you must clearly know where you want to end up."[1]

Covey refers to this goal-oriented mind-set as "Success Habit #2: Begin with the End in Mind." It refers to the strategy of never beginning anything before determining the desired end result.

At the age of seventeen, well before Covey's book was written, I first became aware of the importance of this concept. I had won the competition to become drum major of my high school marching band. As such I would lead the 128 member unit in its football game half-time shows. In addition, I was also given the responsibility of creating each show's theme and formations, plotting out where each member was to march during each tune, plus train the band members each maneuver in practice.

In preparation for this opportunity, during the preceding summer I attended a drum-major training school. The headmaster stated what he believed to be the most important strategy for a successful half-time program. He said, "Focus on the beginning and ending. Make sure those two elements are done well. This is what the people will most remember."

As I created each show and trained the band, I particularly concentrated on the first and last formations. That year the band received rave reviews and wild enthusiasm over the performances.

Since that time, I have endeavored to make this thinking a mind-set of my life. In everything that I do, I attempt to have a good beginning and ending—whether it is delivering a speech, eating a meal, having a family outing, or even going about my daily routines. As a result, not only does my life have more enjoyment, but the things that I do have a greater emotional impact and create lasting impressions.

Power Point

"Start with a clear understanding of your destination."

–Stephen Covey

Earl Nightingale believes that this is one reason why goal setting is so important: "People with goals succeed because they know where they're going."[2]

By implementing this "end-in-mind thinking" as a regular part of your planning and execution of activities, your life will take on a new dimension of power and impact.

Power Point Question

Before you begin something, have you clearly defined how to begin and where you want to end?

———————

"I make known the end from the beginning."
—Isaiah 46:10 (NIV)

News Headline EXTRA! EXTRA!

Cities Finding Gold In Parking Fees And Fines

For many municipalities, revenues from parking fees and fines now rival property taxes as a major source of income.

These cities are not really finding gold in their parking meters. However, they are discovering a great source of extra income. Businesses across the globe are doing the same. They are discovering that they can create great sources of additional income by adding goods and/or services to their already existing product offerings.

As an example, after a trial study, Hilton Hotels installed mini-bars in all their rooms. The corporation found that guests who used their mini-bar units spent an average of $3.40/night. Soon the hotel chain was making more than $14 million in annual sales from its mini-bars with a profit margin of around 38 percent. That came to approximately 5.32 million extra dollars.[1]

This hotel chain was effectively using a powerful income-enhancing strategy that I refer to as "product-added increase."

PRODUCT-ADDED INCREASE

Product-added increase is based on the concept that by piggybacking new products or offerings with existing products or offerings, additional sales and profits can be created.

For instance, years ago, when I was operating my Chrysler dealership in Southern California, I used this strategy. Realizing that we needed to create sources of income in addition to our normal profits from car sales and service, I utilized piggybacking.

After some investigating, I found that there were some optional services we could make available to our customers at the time of sale. These would help the customer and also produce extra income for us. Soon we were offering extended warranties, life and accident insurance policies, and vehicle service contracts. The income from these extra offerings became significant. In fact, there were some months when the extra profits from these offerings made the difference between the dealership being in the black or the red.

I have noticed this product-added strategy being used by many airline reservation agents when they ask if they can also assist with car rental reservations. That simple question produces thousands of dollars in extra income for the airlines every year.

Power Point

"By 'piggybacking,' additional sales and profits can be created."
—Stephen Covey

My friend Peter Lowe—who is billed as "America's Premiere Success Seminar Conductor" —uses this strategy. He added a VIP seating section and celebrity lunches, thereby increasing his profits per seminar.

You, also, may be able to increase your profits by adding extra products and/or services to your line-up.

Power Point Question

How could the strategy of piggybacking increase your profits?

"I am the Lord thy God which teacheth thee to profit."
—Isaiah 48:17

News Headline — EXTRA! EXTRA!

Final Edition

Governor Says "Thanks" To Firms

The governor of a Midwestern state returned from a two-day trip to the Northeast. He traveled there to personally thank the executives of four major companies for their economic investments in the state.

Achievers must be very careful that they do not get so busy and focused on achieving that they forget to be grateful and thankful. Because of demanding schedules, and the hustle of daily routines, it is easy to overlook the thoughtful, productive, and caring acts of others.

How important is it to praise the performance of subordinates? Consider the words of Charles Schwab, who was paid $1 million (back when a million dollars was really worth a million) to run the nation's largest steel empire: "I consider my ability to arouse enthusiasm among people the greatest asset that I possess. The way to develop the best that is in people is by showing appreciation and encouragement."[1]

Zig Ziglar agrees: If you will give everyone the recognition and rewards they deserve, he says, "then [you] have taken a giant stride in becoming Top Performers."[2]

Bill Marriott, the president of Marriott Hotels, also believes in the power of encouragement. He says, "The two most important words in human relations are thank you."[3]

Make gratitude a part of your motivational arsenal. A personal note is such a tool. Rich DeVoss, cofounder of Amway Corporation, believes "people can accomplish great things when they are encouraged by positive and hope-filled messages."[4]

It takes only about three minutes to write a note, fold it, and stick it in an envelope, but the power of that note can be awesome. Personal notes build relationships, which are the most important element in any business.

Also, people who send thank you notes are thought of as gracious, and well-mannered. Additionally, since so few people send them, doing so puts you as a clear cut above the rest.[5]

Here are some keys for better showing appreciation.

HOW TO BETTER SHOW APPRECIATION

1. SAY THANKS NOW: Form the habit of verbalizing appreciation the moment it is appropriate.

2. ACKNOWLEDGE THE CONTRIBUTIONS OF OTHERS: Give unexpected recognition—gifts, flowers, or notes of appreciation—even when there is not a special occasion.

3. CELEBRATE THE SUCCESS OF OTHERS: On special occasions, do something a little extra for people. When someone experiences something out of the ordinary emotionally, it creates an "emotional implantation" on the brain. This experience becomes an interpreter of future thoughts and actions. By spending a little extra time and money celebrating other's special moments,

> **Power Point**
>
> The two most important words in human relations are thank you.
>
> –Bill Marriott

you can bless them. In addition, you create positive imaging of yourself, your company, and/or your product.

Make being grateful one of your success strategies. Be more concerned with how you treat people then how you impress them. You and others will be happier and have more productive days.

Power Point Question

How can you better show appreciation for your family and staff members who have helped you in some way?

"Be ye thankful."
—Colossians 3:15

News Headline

Man Gets Free Trip To Hawaii By Jogging

A Phoenix man revealed that he makes money while jogging. As he runs, he picks up coins lying on the sidewalks and streets. Having found over $5,000 in loose change, he used some of the money to pay for a vacation in Hawaii for his wife and himself.

Many people believe that to experience increase, they must discover, do, or win something big. In reality, great increase often comes as a result of faithfully doing the things that might seem small or insignificant.

Such is the case with Tim Storey. Tim is an in-demand motivational speaker and founder of the Hollywood Bible Study, which regularly attracts over 500 celebrities and movie industry personnel for evenings of learning and inspiration. Tim spoke at one of my Increase Events at which he made this statement: "You will find that the big things in life are normally found in the middle of the little things."

WHERE TO FIND THE BIG THINGS

Several years ago, Tim was working with The Power Team. The Team was a group of bodybuilders who performed onstage feats at school assemblies and convention centers across the nation. They combined their acts with motivational and/or spiritual messages. Tim was in charge of grocery shopping, pressing uniforms, stacking ice, buying water bottles, and so forth. He stated that he was diligent, faithful, and always did the best he could.

One day, as he was walking through the lobby of a hotel, a nationally renowned minister spotted him and called him over to visit. The minister was so impressed with Tim's attitude and apparent good work ethic that he hired him. Soon Tim was traveling around the world as this man's personal assistant.

On one particular trip, the minister could not make it to one of his overseas meetings. The minister called Tim and informed him he would have to be the speaker at the meeting. Tim found himself addressing a crowd of over 18,000 people. He says, "That day, I realized—I wasn't a water boy anymore."

Now, Tim travels all over the world and is greatly impacting our generation. It all began because, while he was faithfully doing the little things, something big appeared.

Faithfulness is a learned behavior. It is a habit pattern of achievers that begins when they honor their commitments, tend to details, and always do the best job possible in all that they set their hands to do.

Power Point

"Big things...are normally found in the middle of...little things."

—Tim Storey

For instance, as I mentioned earlier, I once asked my friend Peter Lowe how he came to put on the largest success seminars in the world. He responded, "I put on the best small seminars in the world."

By better activating this strategy, you may not only get a free trip to Hawaii, but you will also experience greater increase throughout your life.

Power Point Question

How good are you at handling details and taking care of the little things?

"He that is faithful in that which is least is faithful also in much."
—Luke 16:10

News Headline

Final Edition *EXTRA! EXTRA!*

Woman Trapped In Elevator For Three Days

A Hong Kong woman was trapped in a broken elevator for three days before she was discovered and freed. After 60 hours, she emerged hungry, thirsty, and tired.

My friend Aaron Lewis had a fearful incident involving people who were trapped.

Early one bitterly cold winter morning, he was driving home with his two youngest children. The kids had gone with him as he drove his wife, Tiwanna, to the downtown Hartford hospital where she worked.

He told me the story of what happened next. "The snow was six inches high, and I realized that I could not drive all the way into my driveway. The garage was only a few feet away, so I figured that I would leave the little ones in the car as I grabbed a shovel out of the garage in order to clear a path in the driveway. I left the engine running so that the kids would not get too cold.

"Within seconds, my two-year-old son, Israel, had unstrapped himself and locked the automatic door locks. "I pleaded with my son, "Unlock that door now or I am going to give you a spanking.' He yelled back, 'No, no, no.'

"To make matters worse, my son then reached over and turned the heat in the car to the highest setting. I became afraid that this would make his little sister, Madonna, ill. Next, he cranked the radio volume up high. Then he started the windshield wipers. After that, he activated the blinkers and the signal lights.

"Fearing that he might put the car in gear during his antics, I ran into the house to find the extra key. I could not find it anywhere.

"Racing back to the car, nightmarish possibilities of negative outcomes whirled through my head. I was now beginning to panic. If anything happened to those small children, it would be my fault. Government authorities might take the kids away from us due to neglect. I might end up in jail."

THE ANSWER IS WITHIN YOU

Aaron continued, "Then I stopped, took a deep breath, and said a simple prayer: "Father, help me to find an answer.' Suddenly, I heard within me a voice saying, 'The answer is within you.'

"It was then I became aware that the key I needed was not necessarily a physical key. Maybe it was a mental key—a strategy. Then the answer came to me.

"I calmly made a deal with my son, saying, 'If you open the door for daddy, he will give you a candy.' He reached over and unlocked the door."

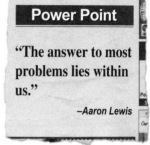

Power Point

"The answer to most problems lies within us."

–Aaron Lewis

Aaron believes that "throughout life, there will be challenging situations. We will conquer most of our battles if we realize that the answer to most problems lies within us."

Power Point Question

How can the principle in this story help you to better solve problems?

———————

"You teach me wisdom in the inmost place."
—Psalm 51:6 (NIV)

News Headline

Dallas Cowboys Coach Was Pure Class

Tom Landry, who coached in an NFL record 20 consecutive winning seasons and led the Dallas Cowboys to two Super Bowl Championships, passed away at the age of 75.

Tom Landry was a living legend. More than any other person, he helped to establish the image of the Cowboys as "America's Team."

Years ago, I had the opportunity of speaking with him at a success seminar in El Paso, Texas. We rode together in the limo to the airport and discussed what Tom had taught that day;

THREE KEYS TO CREATING A WINNING TEAM

1. KNOW YOUR OBJECTIVE: "You must have a clear-cut, well-defined objective. Very few people really know what they want."

2. HAVE AN ACTION PLAN: "Setting a goal is not the main thing. It is deciding how you will go about achieving it. This plan must be written and measurable."

3. IDENTIFY YOUR RESISTANCE: "There will always be forces of resistance released against your action plan. The purpose of these forces is to keep you from accomplishing your objective."

In teaching about resistant forces, Tom went beyond the success strategies that are normally taught, such as setting goals, staying motivated, and remaining positive. He believed that, because they fail to identify the forces of resistance that are working against them, many teams, as well as people and companies, are defeated. Once resistant forces, plans or plays are identified, then strategies can be developed to overcome—or at least minimize—their effectiveness.

Tom thought in terms of defense. He became defensive player and coach for the New York Giants when he was only twenty-nine years old. Since he was young, he could not establish his authority based on age or experience. Also, others had more athletic talent and football skill than he did, so that could not be his foundation, either.

Tom became a specialist in understanding the defenses of other teams. He would spend countless hours learning about opposing players and teams. He devoured anything and everything he could find concerning football.

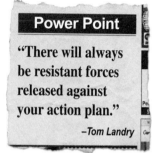

Power Point

"There will always be resistant forces released against your action plan."

–*Tom Landry*

Tom stated, "A leader doesn't have to be the smartest member of a group, but he does need to demonstrate a mastery of his field. Mastery means more than just knowing data and facts; it requires an understanding of the information and the ability to apply that information to the situation at hand."

In the vehicle that day, Tom explained, "A successful leader must be one step ahead of the crowd. Knowledge of resistant forces, combined with proper preparation, enables one to be innovative and overcome opposition."

Power Point Question

Have you identified the resistant forces working against your action plans?

"Wise men lay up knowledge."
—Proverbs 10:14

News Headline

EXTRA! EXTRA!

Final Edition

Can Found Inside Of Fish

A Norwegian fisherman had a surprise when he cut open the codfish that he had caught. Inside of the fish's stomach was a soda can.

You are on the road to greater success if, inside of you, are "cans." The cans that I am referring to are positive affirmations that come out of your inner being in response to challenges, problems, or negative situations.

"WE ARE WELL ABLE"

There is a great story in the Bible about how the lack of a can-do attitude dramatically affected a large group of people. The tribe of Israel had escaped from the bondage of Egypt and arrived on the banks of the Jordan River. Their leader, Moses, sent twelve spies to report on the conditions in the Promised Land.

Ten spies returned with negative reports about the land. These spies focused on the obstacles—walled cities, giants, and the fact that they were outnumbered—and all the reasons why they did not believe they could conquer and win. They exclaimed, "We are not able" (Numbers 13:31 NKJV).

The other two spies, Joshua and Caleb, saw the same challenges. However, they declared that the obstacles didn't matter because the God who had brought the people out of the bondage of Egypt and parted the Red Sea was with them. They announced, "We are well able" (Numbers 13:30).

The ten spies and the people choose to accept the reasons why they could not conquer and win. Therefore, they never entered into the land that God had provided for them. On the other, forty years later, Joshua and Caleb led the people's children to the Promised Land, and they possessed it.

The main difference between Joshua and Caleb and the other spies was a can-do attitude.

Motivational speaker Les Brown concurs: "You must know within yourself that if others can overcome and live their dreams, then so can you."[1] Many times, it is not the problems that you face that make the big difference; it is your attitude toward them. Remember that...

INCREASE COMES IN CANS

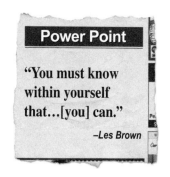

Power Point

"You must know within yourself that...[you] can."

–Les Brown

If you think you are beaten, you are;
If you think you dare not, you don't.
If you like to win, but you think you can't,
It is almost certain you won't.

If you think you'll lose, you've lost,
For out of the world you'll find
Increase begins with a fellow's believing –
It's all in his state of mind.

If you think you are outclassed, you are;
You've got to think higher to rise.
You've got to believe in yourself before
You can ever win the prize.

Life's battles don't always go
To the stronger or faster man;
But sooner or later, the man who wins
Is the man WHO THINKS HE CAN!
-Unknown

Power Point Question

How could you get more "cans" to come out of your mouth?

"We are well able to overcome."
—Numbers 13:30

News Headline — EXTRA! EXTRA!
Final Edition

Postal Truck Plunges Into Pool

When a U.S. Postal Service driver apparently forgot to secure the brakes of his vehicle, the truck rolled down a hill, crashed through a fence and plunged into a residential pool. It was estimated that at least 1,800 pieces of mail were in the water.

Checks belonging to you might not be going to the bottom of a pool, but they could be going to the bottom of someone's pockets. If there are areas in your personal and/or business life in which you are vulnerable to breaches of security, this could be happening to you. How costly this vulnerability can be is demonstrated by the following true story.

"We are short $90,000 in parts inventory!" is what a worried Toyota dealer told Bill Ellis in an urgent phone call. Bill, who was the president of a sales audit company, immediately scheduled an appointment at the dealership to review the records of its service department.

He found that more than a thousand tickets for automotive parts sales were missing. He then discovered that an employee who sold parts was throwing away numerous sales tickets for cash items each week and pocketing the money.

The amazing thing was that the dealership had instituted a program to prevent this kind of theft. A dedicated and loyal employee in accounting had been assigned the task of keeping a Missing Parts Ticket Log.

Then how did this loss occur? Unbelievable as it may seem, the accounting employee had never been instructed in what to do when she discovered that there were missing tickets. She just faithfully noted the missing ticket numbers in a log.

Even more startling is what Bill discovered over the next sixty days. Fresh with the memory of this embezzlement, he audited more than a hundred other dealerships, specifically checking for missing parts sales tickets. To his surprise, he found the following:

ARE YOU INVITING THEFT?

1. One-fifth (20%) of the dealerships had no system to record ticket numbers at all.

2. One-third (33%) of the dealerships allowed the same person who received cash from customers to keep track of missing tickets.

Power Point

"People do what is inspected, not what is expected."

–*Bob Harrison*

3. And, most amazingly, not one—yes, not one—of the hundred dealerships audited had checked their Missing Ticket Log Report in the previous three months.

Every one of these businesses was inviting theft and embezzlement because they either did not have, or did not maintain, a proper inspection system.

You may think that you could never have this kind of problem, but consider the fact that even Jesus did. John 12:6 states that Judas, one of Jesus' twelve disciples, served as treasurer, of the disciples, and that "he was a thief; as keeper of the money bag, he used to help himself to what was put into it" (NIV). If Jesus was susceptible to embezzlement, then so are you.

As I teach in my Time Increase CD series, "People do what is inspected, not what is expected."

Even if you have faithful and loyal employees, not have inspection systems invites looseness that can result in significant losses.

Power Point Question

What systems do you have in place to protect the key areas of income, expenses, cash flow, customer data, and inventory?

"Riches can disappear fast…so watch your business interests
closely."
—Proverbs 27:23-24 (TLB)

Eastman Curtis is a gifted speaker who specializes in motivating high school and college students. One day he need more than a cow costume to attract attention at a school. He needed a strategy in order to turn around a negative situation.

Eastman was scheduled to speak to a college assembly right after the students' lunch break. He had brought two young men with him who were former world champion tag-team kickboxers. As they walked into the assembly center, they were startled to find that there were only three people in the auditorium. At one of my Increase Events in Florida, Eastman shared how he dramatically changed the situation.

"I was not willing to accept the empty auditorium. Knowing that students had to be around somewhere, I called my two kickboxer friends over and said, 'Come on, I've got a plan.' Rushing over to the school cafeteria, we found it cram-packed with humanity.

"I jumped up onto a chair and yelled, 'Hey! Attention! Can I have your attention, please? For today, and today only, we have with us two former world champion kickboxers! They are about to put on a kickboxing exhibition you won't want to miss, right now in the auditorium. Follow me.'

"Several of the students started screaming, 'Yeahhh!' As we left the cafeteria, I felt like the Pied Piper! I looked behind me and saw that there were at least a hundred students following us.

CREATING MOTION

"These two friends of mine, who hadn't practiced kick boxing in years, went on stage and just started beating the mess out of each other. Knowing that a fight will draw a crowd every time, I left the doors open, cranked up the PA system to its maximum and started yelling, 'FIGHT! FIGHT! THERE'S A FIGHT IN HERE!' More people started running to the auditorium from everywhere. Soon the place was packed. Then, when my friends were done, I quickly got up and shared my message."

Power Point

"A body in motion tends to stay in motion."

–Isaac Newton

Eastman activated a powerful success strategy that is based upon a law of physics given by Isaac Newton: "A body in motion tends to stay in motion."

Anthony Robbins believes this strategy is a key ingredient of achievers: "Successful people…kept asking, kept trying."[1] The great Oklahoma comedian, Will Rogers once said, "Even if you are on the right track, you will get run over if you just sit there."

If you find yourself in what looks like a subpar situation, think about how you can begin to put things in "motion" to create a turnaround.

Power Point Question

How can "creating motion" better enable you to overcome?

———————————

"Be strong and do not give up, for your work will be rewarded."
—2 Chronicles 15:7 (NIV)

News Headline

Final Edition

EXTRA! EXTRA!

Plane That Crashed Was On Autopilot

The safety board's report on the commuter passenger plane that crashed in Buffalo, New York revealed that the aircraft was on autopilot when it went down in icy weather.

For a captain to allow a plane to be on autopilot during inclement weather violates federal safety recommendations. In some ways, running a business is much like flying a plane. When conditions are favorable, things can kind of run on autopilot. However, when conditions have deteriorated, one needs to take charge—and do it quickly.

My friend, Ed Gungor, shared on this subject at one of my Increase Events in Hawaii. Ed is a *New York Times* best-selling author, seminar speaker, and pastor.

IS IT OUR WORK OR GOD'S SOVEREIGNTY?

People tend to fall in one ditch or the other. Some folks end up in the ditch of thinking that little work will be required in order to achieve success. They live their lives just waiting for some kind of increase to happen. They think that increase is all God and His sovereign blessing. God can do whatever He wants to. It would be a simple matter for Him to make them win some kind of Divine lottery.

On the other hand, there are others who believe that it's all about their own efforts and cunning. They may say that God brings the increase to them because it makes for good religious press. However, they really don't trust God for increase—they create enough of it on their own.

God does value planning, effort, and work. He views the talents and abilities He gives us as investments...and He expects a return. The young man in Matthew 25 who heard, 'Well done good and faithful servant,' was the guy who worked with what had been invested in him! On the other hand, the one who heard, 'You wicked and lazy servant,' was into heavy sovereignty – believing that he could 'reap where he had not sown.' God was pretty torqued at that guy—he was a slacker.

Psalm 20:7 declares, "Some trust in chariots and some in horses, but we trust in the name of the Lord our God." You would think that if Israel was not to trust in the chariots and horses, then why have them? Or, if they have them, why not have some old, beat up ones? But Israel had the best chariots and horses that money could buy.

Power Point

"Be willing to re-imagine how things work in God's world."

—*Ed Gungor*

Here is the key: They had the best, but they refused to trust in the best. I believe that is what God wants from us—to do our best, be our best, and strive to get better, but never trust in that; always trust Him.

I heard a story about a rancher who was showing his pastor around his place with its immaculate buildings, well maintained fences, and manicured lawns. The pastor commented piously how God had blessed the property. The rancher replied, "You should have seen it when He had it all by himself."

The secret is balance. Do all you can and then believe God to make up what you cannot do.

Power Point Question

How well do you balance work and sovereignty?

"He that is slothful…is brother to him that is a great waster."
—Proverbs 18:9

News Headline

Vegetarians Becoming Flexitarians

Many people are becoming part-time vegetarians. The American Dialect Society calls them "Flexitarians."

I believe in being a "flexitarian"—not just in terms of diet, but also as a mindset for living.

Flexibility, or the willingness to adapt and change, is a key element for success in any arena of life. Noted author and playwright George Bernard Shaw stated, "Progress is impossible without change."[1]

Yet there is a challenge. Change, by itself, can be disastrous. Any successful endeavor must have some form of structure, or it leads to chaos and uncertainty. On the other side of the coin, structure without the attitude of change leads to stagnation and eventual death. Therefore, in every situation, one must find a balance between structure and flexibility.

With that understanding, here is the key to the successful utilization of the mind-set of change: Recognize that change is not a concept just to be ingrained into long-range planning. To be really effective, flexibility must be integrated into one's daily routine.

For instance, each day, I have plans, schedules and/or appointments. My day has a pre-planned flow to it, but I live my life ready to adjust or alter my plans as new opportunities appear or circumstances change. I realize, as I have often stated, that "God cannot effectively use—or bless—anyone who is not willing to be interrupted." This strategy allows me to continually be open to fresh input and to "seize" the best for any given day and for my life in general.

In the biblical story about the farmer Elisha, the flexibility mind-set is demonstrated. Because he had this perspective, he embraced a major career change. In the story, Elisha was in his field, plowing away. (I am sure that he had set a plan for how many furrows he would plow that day.) Then the prophet Elijah walked by and called him to join him. The Bible states, "He left the oxen and ran after Elijah" (I Kings 19:20). Because he was willing to quickly change his actions, he was able to seize the opportunity!

Here are some keys that have helped me to be a "change maker":

1. STABILITY: I strive for stability, permanence and structure. However, I recognize that only eternal things are really permanent.

2. ATTITUDE: I think of changes not as inconveniences, but as new adventures.

Power Point

The number one ingredient we have seen in successful operations is flexibility."[3]

–Jacquelyn Wonder, coauthor, The Flexibility Factor

3. READINESS: I live ready to change. Thinking of potential changes in advance, I develop action plans to deal with the opportunities if they occur.

4. TIMING: Although one can alter one's path at almost any time, some moments are more favorable for doing so than others. I attempt to be sensitive to what's going on so that I can perceive the right moment to make changes.

5. RAPID RESPONSE: When an opportunity that demands change occurs, I move quickly. Speed is often the difference between success and a missed opportunity.

John H. Patterson once said, "Only fools and dead men don't change their minds. Fools won't. Dead men can't."[2] Determine to make yourself more flexible and ready for positive change.

Power Point Question

How well do you anticipate and/or adjust for changes?

"And he left the oxen and ran."
—I Kings 19:20 (NKJV)

News Headline

Doorman Refuses To Hail Cab

A doorman at a luxury New York City hotel refused to get a taxi for a vacationing couple who were hotel guests. He told them to "take a hike."

The doorman's attitude may sound like the height of rudeness and insensitivity. Actually, he was being considerate. When the couple asked for a cab, he informed them that their destination was only two blocks away and that they could save both time and the cab fare by walking. The couple gave the doorman a good tip and took a nice stroll.

An occasional walk might benefit a person only a little, but regular exercise can have great benefits. "According to the Centers for Disease Control and Prevention (CDC), more than 60 percent of all Americans do not get enough exercise. About 25 percent don't exercise at all."[1]

"Exercise has been proven to help with weight management, improve skeletal-muscle strength and endurance, cardiopulmonary fitness, flexibility, and possibly improve your immune system and mental health. Exercising twice weekly has been shown to reduce the threat of strokes by 40 percent, coronary heart disease by 15 percent."[2]

THE BENEFITS OF REGULAR EXERCISE

Years ago, Dr. Kenneth Cooper began an intensive study of exercise. He discovered that people who exercised regularly had physical and medical improvements. However, he also found that if a person's exercise program was directed toward only muscle building, the individual rarely achieved good physical fitness.

In his best-selling book *Aerobics*, he explained the difference: "The key to fitness is oxygen. In the body, the fuel is food, and the flame is oxygen. The body can store food, but it can't store oxygen. As one increases his oxygen capability, he increases his endurance and overall fitness."[3]

Dr. Cooper then created an exercise program that focused on this element. "Aerobics is that form of exercise which forces the body to consume increased amounts of oxygen and as such is the only form of exercise that benefits not just the skeletal muscles but the whole body."[4]

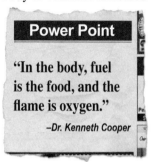

Power Point

"In the body, fuel is the food, and the flame is oxygen."

–Dr. Kenneth Cooper

My mother, Edna Harrison-Harlin, was a person who believed in the benefits of regular exercise. When she was ninety years old, she would still swim thirty laps in her home association's pool three times a week. People could not believe her age as she drove around in her convertible so happy and healthy.

A good exercise exercise program need not take a lot of time. "Three 10-minute bouts of activity can be as effective a cardiovascular workout as one 30-minute session," says Dr. Edward Laskowski, codirector of the Sports Medicine Center at the Mayo Clinic.[5]

Add years to your life, and increase your vitality and alertness, by having a regular exercise regimen.

Power Point Question

In what ways would your productivity and enjoyment of life increase if you were more physically fit?

Beloved, I wish above all things that thou…be in health."
—3 John 2

According to the reports, the man because suspicious when food began to disappear from his kitchen. He then installed a hidden camera and turned it on when he went to work.

It seems ironic that the man would not have noticed food disappearing sooner. However, even more amazing to me is that so many achievers do not notice time, as well as money, disappearing because they do not delegate adequately. I recently addressed this topic in a different Power Point. However, good delegation is so vital in order for you to experience increase that I wanted to revisit the issue.

In order to maximize your efficiency, there are times when you must have others assist you. They can do the tasks that would prevent you from spending time on your most important and/or desirable tasks. Failing to do so will cause you to be less effective and more stressed out.

When you delegate, "you will achieve more results than you ever thought possible. You will have more time for managerial activities. You will find yourself focusing on doing a few tasks very well rather than doing a lot of things poorly."[1]

A good biblical example of a challenge to delegate can be found in the life of Moses. When his father-in-law, Jethro, saw him trying to serve as the sole judge for the Israelites and solve innumerable disputes and legal questions, he told him,

> Both you and these people who are with you will surely wear
> yourselves out. For this thing is too much for you; you are not

able to perform it by yourself...Moreover you shall select from all the people able men...Every great matter they shall bring to you, but every small matter they themselves shall judge. So it will be easier for you, for they will bear the burden with you.
—Exodus 18:18, 21-22 NKJV

Moses heeded this advice. "[He] chose able men...and made them heads over the people" (Exodus 18:25 NKJV).

Here are some of my favorite quotes on the subject of delegating:

"Every day, I ask myself, "What am I doing that can be done by someone else?"

—John Maxwell[2]

"My secret is that I get things out of my hands and into someone else's." —David Ingles[3]

"Never do anything that someone else can do for you, as well or better." —Raymond Johnson[4]

"When you start running out of time, pay someone to give you more."

—Joyce Meyer[5]

> **Power Point**
>
> "What [are you] doing that can be done by someone else?"
> *–John Maxwell*

Over the next few weeks, practice delegating more. However, be sure to set up inspection systems. Not having follow-up systems is where many achievers have gotten "burned" while attempting to delegate. As I said earlier, quoting from my Time Increase CD series, "People do what is inspected, not what is expected."

Power Point Question

How could better delegation improve your productivity?

————————

"You are not able to perform it by yourself."
—Exodus 18:18 (NKJV)

News Headline
Final Edition
EXTRA! EXTRA!

Dead Woman Gets Job Back

A woman died while going to a hearing to fight her job dismissal. Authorities said the woman was revived by paramedics. She has fully recovered and was reinstated to her job.

M any women experience a sense of "dying" at certain times in their lives—an emotional death. For example, when the youngest child goes off to college, gets married, or just moves out on her or her own, a mother may believe that her role of nurturing and mentoring has ended. Some people respond to this vacuum by indulging in a life of new activities, as exemplified by the following poem:

> In the dim and distant past,
> When life's tempo wasn't fast,
> Grandma used to rock and knit,
> Crochet, tat and baby-sit.
> When the kids were in a jam,
> They could always count on Gram.
> In an age of gracious living,
> Grandma was the gal for giving.
>
> Grandma now is at the gym,
> Exercising to keep slim.
> She's off touring with the bunch,
> Or taking clients out to lunch.
> Going north to ski or curl,
> All her days are in a whirl.
> Nothing seems to stop or block her,
> Now that Grandma's off her rocker!
>
> —Unknown

Others, however, are discovering a new source of joy and excitement by mentoring their grandchildren. Such is the case with Arvella Schuller, wife of Dr. Robert Schuller, who is pastor of the Crystal Cathedral located in Southern California. Arvella produces the *Hour of Power* television program, handles all the family's personal finances, has a speaking career, and does volunteer work.

MAKING GRANDCHILDREN A PRIORITY

Yet despite her busy schedule, Arvella has chosen to make her family —especially her fifteen grandchildren—a priority. She says, "A changing world can be a hurting and lonely world unless we see ourselves as comforters, companions and counselors of those we love."[1]

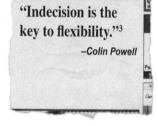

Power Point

"Indecision is the key to flexibility."[3]

–Colin Powell

Arvella regularly schedules time to give undivided attention to each grandchild. If one has a special need, she will be there regardless of her busy schedule.

My friend Betty Southard coauthored a book entitled *The Grandmother Book*. In it, she states, "Kids need to know that there is someone, beyond their parents, who loves them in a very special way. A grandparent's love and understanding complements the love they get from their parents."[2]

Arvella believes that one of the most valuable things that a grandparent can do is to release their love, knowledge, wisdom, experience, and prayers into the lives of the younger generation.

Even if you do not have children or grandchildren, there are probably young people around you who would greatly benefit from having some of your love and attention. Why not make a difference in someone's life?

Power Point Question

How can you adjust your priorities or schedule in order to better mentor and influence your grandchildren or others of the younger generation?

"The aged women…may teach the young women."
—Titus 2:3

News Headline

Saboteurs Derail Train

An Amtrak train jettisoned off a 30-foot high bridge into a dry stream bed. Several cars plunged from the bridge at 50 mph, coming to rest lying sideways on the sandy bottom of the desert wash.

The removal of twenty-nine spikes from the tracks by saboteurs caused the train to crash. Likewise, with achievers, seemingly little things, such as poor personal work habits, can cause personal and professional derailment.

Best-selling author Stephen Covey believes that derailment can happen when one does not clearly distinguish the difference between what is important and what is urgent. He says, "The problem is that when urgency becomes the dominant factor in our lives, then importance is not. Urgency itself is not the problem. The problem is that we can get so caught up in doing, we do not stop and ask if what we are doing really needs to be done."[1]

Covey believes that "effective management is putting first things first. While leadership decides what the 'first things' are, it is management that puts them first, day-to-day, moment-by-moment. This requires one to operate by values rather than by impulse or the desire of a given moment."[2]

Here are some strategies that I have learned for staying on track:

STAYING ON TRACK

1. STAY FOCUSED: Momentum is achieved not in the switchyard of multiple choices but on a single tack heading toward a predetermined destination.

2. WATCH THE DETAILS: Do you regularly check and inspect the small but important areas of your business and life? The removal of a few rail spikes can derail an entire train.

3. MAKE YOUR CARGO MORE VALUABLE: Don't just say on track financially. Live a morally consistent life. Private victories lead to a life of public impact and influence.

4. WRITE A DAILY PLAN: Without a plan for each day, you can easily get distracted handling the seemingly most urgent tasks rather than the most important ones. Write out or create in your computer a daily "To Do" list based on what is truly important.

Power Point

"Effective management is putting first things first."

–Stephen Covey

5. MAINTAIN BALANCE: Give time and attention to all the important areas of your life: physical, family, financial, intellectual, social, professional, and spiritual. If a train gets too far off balance, it will overturn. So will you.

6. REWARD YOURSELF: At the end of a specific task or assignment, reward yourself by doing or making something you enjoy.

7. MAINTAIN PROPER FUEL LEVELS: Eat properly, exercise regularly, and get enough sleep. Also, infuse your life with spiritual power. Spend time spent reading the Bible, praising and worshipping God, and/or engaging in personal meditation.

The desired outcome of a goal-oriented life is to arrive at one's desired destination as quickly and efficiently as possible. Implementing the above strategies can help you stay on track and avoid being derailed and ending up at the bottom of a ditch.

Power Point Question

What are you doing to prevent personal and professional derailment?

———————

"Turn not from it [God's will] to the right hand or to the left,
that thou mayest prosper whithersoever thou goest."
—Joshua 1:7

A Pittsburg man was not searching in caves, and he did not have a metal detector. However, when it seemed as if his life was dead in water, old jewelry helped him to find a whole new direction for his life.

For several years, I spoke at seminars with Dr. Edwin Louis Cole. Dr. Cole, who is now deceased, was a master at reaching out and helping men with their unique challenges concerning sex, marriage, and money. At some of these seminars, he shared the story of this man, who had a whole new life emerge out of a negative event.

The man had worked at a steel mill for twenty-two years. Unexpectedly, the mill was shut down, and he found himself with no job, no retirement funds, and unemployment pay that was running out. As the days and weeks passed with no apparent solution, tension mounted within him, and the former steelworker became depressed and irritable. He started going for long walks to get out of the house and to occupy himself.

CREATING GOOD OUT OF BAD SITUATIONS

One evening, a bad snowstorm hit the city. The next day, he went for his customary walk and noticed a neighbor looking out her window. Realizing that, because of the snow, she could not get out of her house, he stopped and offered to shovel the snow away from her doors and sidewalk. She offered to pay him, but he refused to take any money for his help.

The next day, another neighbor, who had seen the good job that he had done, offered to pay him to shovel her sidewalk. Seeing an opportunity, he used this money to buy shovels for both himself and his sons, who began to shovel snow for people after school. When spring came, the woman asked him if he would clean her backyard and attic. She informed him that he could just throw everything away. He took home some of the jewelry, appliances, and other things that were to be discarded, cleaned and/or fixed them up, and sold them.

Building upon this idea, he and his boys then started going from house to house asking people if they wanted their yards and attics cleaned. They made money on their labor and in the process, obtained unusual things to sell.

The man told Ed, "Soon I was operating a clean-up business plus an antiques store and was making more money than I ever had at the mill."

Ed concluded by sharing that the man told him, "Getting laid off was the best thing that ever happened to me."

Oftentimes, when facing negative situations, it is best to view the situation the same way a judo master views an attack; he converts the negative energy that is coming against him into a positive force.

Power Point Question

How can you more creatively react to negative events?

_____

"I will give thee the…hidden riches of secret places."
—Isaiah 45:3

News Headline

Globe Littered With Land Mines

It is estimated that the world is littered with 80 to 100 million antipersonnel land mines spread over 64 different countries.

They may look harmless, but the ability of land mines to kill or maim is just a footstep away. The road to success is littered with mines. However, these mines are not buried in the ground. Instead, they can be found in the minds of those individuals who are threatened by change. They normally ignite and explode out of the mouths of their carriers in response to someone suggesting that there is a better way, a different method, another viewpoint, or a need to change.

Donald Trump believes that "life's losers get their sense of accomplishment and achievement from trying to stop others."[1]

In his book, *Peak Performance Principles for High Achievers*, John Noe states that high achievers "must be willing to risk rejection from their peers. If you study the biographies of great people, you will discover that most of them were misunderstood, often by those closest to them."[2] He also says, "They struggled against overwhelming obstacles and labors in the face of sharp criticism."[3]

Here are words and opinions that some high achievers of the past had to face.

VERBAL LAND MINES OF THE PAST

"Drill into the ground to try and find oil? You're crazy."—Workers to Edwin L. Drake, 1859

"The 'telephone' has too many shortcomings to be seriously considered as a means of communication. The device is inherently of no value to us." —Western Union executive memo, 1876

"Heavier-than-air flying machines are impossible."—President, British Royal Society, 1895[4]

"I have determined that there is no market for talking pictures"—Thomas Edison[5]

"I have traveled the length and breadth of this country and talked with the best people, and I can assure you that data processing is a fad that won't last out the year."—Major publisher's book editor, 1957

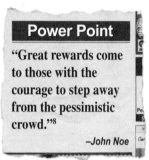

Power Point

"Great rewards come to those with the courage to step away from the pessimistic crowd."[8]

–John Noe

"We don't like their sound...guitar music is on the way out."—Recording company executive, rejecting the Beatles, 1962[6]

"You ain't going nowhere son. You ought to go back to driving a truck." —Grand Old Opry Manager to Elvis Presley[7]

I am not saying that achievers should listen only to those who agree with them. Constructive criticism and wise counsel are extremely valuable and should always be sought after and be highly treasured. However, we must insulate ourselves from the negative, can't-do-it individuals who we may encounter on the road to success.

In the words of the ancient Chinese proverb, "Man who says it cannot be done should not interrupt man who is doing it."

Power Point Question

Are you letting other people's negative words and/or actions keep you from crossing your "field of dreams"?

"And they spread...a bad report."
—Numbers 13:32 (NIV)

News Headline

Final Edition

EXTRA!
EXTRA!

Contest Officials Search For God

A publisher's sweepstakes notice arrived at a Florida Assemblies of God church addressed to "A. God." It notified "him" that he was a finalist for the $11 million top prize.

Florence and Fred Littauer's lives changed when God came to their home.

Florence, along with her husband, conducts marriage seminars and teaches on personality types to church groups, conferences, and conventions nationwide. I have appeared on the same program with them at numerous conferences, and they are always a big hit. Florence's book *Personality Plus* is a classic among those who study personality differences.

After their two brain-damaged sons died, the Littauers found themselves in a desperate search to find their way out of the misery. They wanted to find answers to the unanswered questions in their lives. Florence often shares the story when she speaks.

"We were achieving on the surface, but we were hurting underneath. Fred went to the library and started studying books on religion. We soon came to the realization what our problem was. We needed a spiritual force in control of our lives.

"Before they died, I learned this principle of control through my two brain-damaged sons. Each one had been beautiful to look at—blond hair, dimpled chins, and bright blue eyes. They had eyes, but they could not see; ears, but they could not hear; feet, but they could not walk. They looked all right on the outside, but without a proper functioning brain, with no controlling mechanism, nothing worked right.

"I realized that we were a lot like those boys. We looked all right on the outside, but inside, nothing much was working right."

When Florence and Fred experienced a spiritual renewal in their lives, they received newfound peace and a sense of purpose.

As they continued to study the Bible, they also developed a fresh awareness that not everyone was created by God to function alike. Each person was unique and different. This understanding of uniqueness caused Florence to launch her career of teaching people to recognize, appreciate, and build successful career teams using the personality differences of others.

Power Point

"Appreciate people's differences and build upon them."[3]

–Francis Littauer

Florence maintains that to effectively lead, we must determine that we are not going to let people's differences be an irritation to us. Instead, each of us must learn to appreciate people's differences and build upon them. She teaches, "How people handle their differences with others will largely determine their level of success or failure."

Best-selling author Steven Covey agrees with this approach to life. He teaches, "Valuing the differences of others is the essence of synergy. The person who is truly effective has the humility and reverence to appreciate the rich resources available through interaction with the minds and hearts of other human beings. Those differences add to his knowledge and to his understanding of reality."[1] Steven continues, "Consider ways in which differences might be used as stepping-stones to alternative solutions."[2]

Power Point Question

How can you better use the unique talents, gifts, and opinions of others in your business or family?

"For the body is not one member, but many."
—1 Corinthians 12:14

News Headline

Varmints Stink Up School

For over a month, school teachers and staff members have been grappling with a smelly problem in one of their buildings.

The stench was apparently caused by skunks, who were releasing odors near a drainage system next to one of the classroom complexes.

The "stink posse" at a local elementary school had given up. Apparently, heating intake vents were carrying the skunks' foul smell to all parts of the building. Teachers and students complained of headaches and had difficulty concentrating. Skunk traps were set, but were ineffective, so school officials have decided to hire professionals to combat the "stink invasion."Skunks are not the only things that can stink up your life—negative friends and critical associates can, also. However, when these "stinky varmints" start hanging around, they can cause more than headaches and loss of concentration. They can cause you to experience isolation and hostility.

Dr. Phil McGraw is a best-selling author and television personality. He believes that when one is continually exposed to negative input, they will begin to "choose thoughts that depreciate and demean themselves. They also choose the consequences of low self-esteem and low self-confidence...which are alienation and hostility."[1]

In addition, over time, their "internal dialogue" becomes negative. Dr. Phil defines internal dialogue as the "real-time conversations that you have with yourself about everything that is going on in your life." He believes that "regular exposure to negative internal dialogue, like prolonged exposure to the sun, can over time literally kill a person without them even knowing it. The reason is that they have created for themselves a toxic internal environment."[2]

If negative friends are stinking up your life, you have three options: (1) Choose to continue the relationship and suffer the consequences, (2) try to change their thinking, or (3) separate yourself from, or at least reduce your exposure to, their influence.

The choosing of one's inner circle of friends is one of the most important of all success strategies. Here are what some of my friends and fellow teachers say about those who influence the way we think about ourselves.

THE INFLUENCE OF FRIENDS

"It is not your accomplishments that will make you great, it's who you choose to surround yourself with."—General Norman Schwarzkopf, USA, Retired[3]

"My choice to change my closest friends was a turning point in my life."—John Mason, best-selling author of *An Enemy Called Average*[4]

"To increase, a person must find friends who have strengths they do not possess."—Mark Victor Hansen, best-selling author of *Chicken Soup for the Soul*[5]

"To be a winner you must associate with winners."—Dexter Yager, marketing crown distributor[6]

"Eaglelike folks may be rare, but they possess an incredible loyalty when they link up."—Charles Swindoll, radio personality and author[7]

"True friends are the ones who will be faithful and will keep you in touch with reality."—Colin Powell, former secretary of state[8]

> **Power Point**
>
> "Regular exposure to internal dialogue...can...kill a person."
>
> –Dr. Phil McGraw

"Success comes not from what you know but who you know."—Lee Iacocca, former president of Chrysler Corporation[9]

Make a decision today to carefully choose whom you surround yourself with.

Power Point Question

Do you have friends who are stinking up your life?

"The companion of fools will suffer harm."
—Proverbs 13:20 (NASB)

QSR magazine, a publication for restaurant owners-operators, awarded the restaurant chain for its excellence of operations. The study measured speed, accuracy, menu-board appearance, and speaker clarity.

Back in 1960, Truett Cathy never dreamed that one day he would be operating one of America's largest and most successful fast-food companies. On the contrary, he was facing one of his greatest crises. His second restaurant, The Dwarf House, had burned down. It seemed that his dreams for a successful career in food services had literally gone up in smoke. To make matters worse, that same week, doctors found cancerous polyps in his colon.

These bad circumstances could not stop him, however. He had a confidence in himself and his God.

Truett quickly dealt with, and was able to overcome, his health problems. Soon he was rebuilding the restaurant. Only this time he made it different. He decided to open it as Atlanta's first self-serve fast-food restaurant specializing in chicken.

Sales were mediocre until he made a discovery. By removing the bone and skin from the chicken breast, he could cut the cooking time in half. This could greatly decrease his expenses. He then came up with the idea of putting the breast on a bun and adding special seasonings. The Chick-fil-A sandwich was born and the rest is history. Today, even though every store is closed on Sundays, the more than 1,600 Chick-fil-A outlets across America bring in some of the industry's top sales income per unit.[1]

I had the opportunity to visit with Mr. Cathy in Washington, D.C. He is a happy and gracious man who is very involved with various charities. He shared with me some of the reasons why he believes that "it is easier to succeed than to fail":

IT IS EASIER TO SUCCEED THAN TO FAIL

1. "It's easier to succeed because success eliminates the agony and frustration of defeat."

2. "It's easier to succeed because money spent to fail must be spent again to succeed."

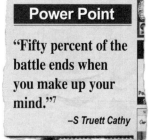

Power Point

"Fifty percent of the battle ends when you make up your mind."[7]

–S Truett Cathy

3. "It's easier to succeed because feelings of discouragement and discontent accompany failure, but joy and excitement come from succeeding."[2]

Mr. Cathy succeeded because he would not let a setback stop him from pursuing his dreams. Robert Schuller concurs with this attitude. He says, "There are black holes surrounding all of us."[3] However, true achievers "are empowered by problems. These people turn every problem into a decision....a decision to overcome."[4] My friend Myles Munroe states, "All leaders, regardless of their abilities...will encounter crises...A crisis is...simply a turning point at which leadership ability is tested and matured. A crisis can lead you to greater challenge and victory."[5] Do you have problems that need to be turned into victories? If so, go for it. In the words of Robert Schuller, "It is better to attempt to do something great and fail than to do nothing and succeed."[6]

Power Point Question

Is there some change in attitude, method, or technique that could bring you increase?

"My yoke is easy, and my burden is light."
—Matthew 11:30

People are willing to pay large sums of money for a seat if they believe that it provides them with a special opportunity to make money, gain prestige, and/or experience great enjoyment.

For instance, in the financial area, not long ago, a seat on the New York Stock Exchange sold for $2.6 million.[1] In the political arena, during the Bill Clinton presidency, it was reported that a seat at the dinner table for a special occasion at the White House could be arranged for those who made a $100,000 donation to "the party."[2]

In the business arena, because of the perceived value of the material being taught, I have known people to pay up to $7,500 for a seat at a success seminar. In the athletic realm, I was speaking in Atlanta while the World Series was being played there, and I heard that because of the people's enthusiasm for the team, the available seats were selling for $1,000 each.

Sometimes, however, a "special seat" becomes available because of reasons other than money. I have experienced several of these occasions in my life. Because of my friendships and speaking venues, I have had the wonderful opportunity to dine, fellowship, and share with some great people such as Margaret Thatcher, George H. W. Bush, Mikhail Gorbachev, Colin Powell, Dr. Robert Schuller, Larry King, Bob Costas, Loretta Scott King, Rudolph Giuliani, Bob Dole, and others.

When these opportunities occur, I make it a point to maximize the experience. Here are some things I have learned about such opportunities that can help to increase your enjoyment and personal impact when you encounter them.

MAXIMIZING ENCOUNTERS WITH WELL-KNOWN PEOPLE

1. PREPARE IN ADVANCE: Study and obtain background information about key VIPs. Think about, and maybe even make notes of, questions to ask during conversations that will better enable you to relax and cherish the experience as well as carry on intelligent dialogue.

Power Point

"Most celebrities love to associate with 'real' people."

–Bob Harrison

2. BE YOURSELF: Most celebrities love to associate with "real" people who are enjoyable to be around.

3. SHOW INTEREST: Maintain focus, show a caring attitude, and be interested in them and what they are sharing.

4. TALK MINIMALLY: Concentrate your conversation on friendly chat—asking for knowledge and/or discovering common points of interest.

5. BE TIME CONSCIOUS: Leaders are normally on tight schedules. They will relax and better enjoy their visit with you if they sense that you respect their time.

6. CAPTURE THE MOMENT: In order to relive the memory of the occasion, obtain programs, pictures, or autographs.

7. BE THANKFUL: Send a note of appreciation to the host(s).

Power Point Question

Which of the above keys can you activate to increase the impact and memories of your special opportunities?

"Mary has chosen what is better [sitting and visiting with Jesus]."
—Luke 10:40, 42 NIV

News Headline

EXTRA!
EXTRA!

Final Edition

Many Still In The Dark

The storm that swept through the state has left 50,000 residents without power and in the dark.

One day James Stovall found himself in the dark. It was not because of a power failure; he had gone blind. The degenerative eye disease that doctors had discovered when he was seventeen had finally taken its toll.

Stovall moved into a nine-by-twelve foot room in the back of his home, having no idea what he would do with the rest of his life. He exclaims, "My whole world had shrunk to that little room. However, after months in that room, I asked myself, 'What is the worst thing that can happen to me if I leave this room?'...None of them seemed as bad as spending the rest of my life there."[1] That day he walked fifty feet to his mail box. There has been no stopping him since. As founder of the Narrative Television Network, every year he produces narrated versions of over one thousand movies and television shows. In addition, he speaks at large events three times a month and has authored twelve books.

At one of my Increase Events, he shared, "I awoke one morning and found that I could not see. Since then, I have discovered that there is a second blindness that many people have. It has nothing to do with a physical problem. It has to do with the fact that most people lack the ability to make any sense out of their lives—to become the people they were created to be.

Stovall said, "I may have lost my sight, but in the aftermath, I gained a greater vision that I ever had before. I choose not to let blindness squelch my ambition...or the pursuit of my personal destiny. I may have lost my sight, but I have gained greater vision than I ever had before. Going blind was the best thing that ever happened to me."[2]

"Sight is a function of the eyes; vision is a function of the heart," Myles Munroe.[3] "[Nothing great] was ever done without...this mysterious force called vision...Vision generates hope in the midst of despair and provides endurance in tribulation...Without vision, life would be a study in cyclic frustration within a whirlwind of despair. Vision is the foundation of courage."[4]

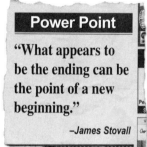

Power Point

"What appears to be the ending can be the point of a new beginning."

–James Stovall

Munroe continues, saying, "Your future is not ahead of you—it lies within you...vision determines your destiny,"[5] and "Vision is the juice of life. It is the prerequisite for passion and the source of persistence. When you have vision, you know how to stay in the race and complete it."[6]

Power Point Question

Do you have a vision for your life?

_____

"Then the eyes of the blind shall be opened."
—Isaiah 35:5

News Headline

EXTRA! EXTRA!

Final Edition

Elevator Suddenly Plunges

An elevator that was overloaded with 17 prisoners and 2 sheriff deputies suddenly took a two-story plunge. When one of the guards closed the door, authorities reported that "the ride from hell started."

When I read the story about the elevator plunging, I recalled occasions some time ago when different sales achievers came to me in desperation because their incomes had unexpectedly taken a "plunge." It was out of those experiences that I began to teach people and companies how to have a more stable base of income by creating customer loyalty. One key way that this is achieved is by maintaining contact with customers in order to get referrals and repeat business.

Years later, I had the opportunity to meet a man who was a master at marketing. Ken Kerr, who has since passed away, and I became friends and often exchanged ideas. He was the creative project director for Walt Disney's Epcot Center. In addition, he developed marketing programs for Sea World and several other corporations.

SUCCESSFUL MARKETING THROUGH REPEAT SALES

Ken believed that the most successful marketing strategies consisted of developing products and programs for repeat sales. He shared the following story on the value of repeat sales at one of my Hawaii Increase Events:

"One of my clients ran a promotion on the internet to sell a collection of coins to new customers for $19. He actually lost a few dollars on every sale. Over 50,000 people responded to the offer.

"The next month, he sent out a follow-up mailing to all those who had purchased the $19-dollar item. Nearly 10,000 of those same people bought an 'after-sale' collection at $1,000 each. My client grossed $2 million on the after-sale of the original offer.

"That's not all. Later, he contacted those 10,000 people who had purchased the after-sale $1,000 collection and gave them an additional offer. About 1,500 of them bought more coins, averaging $5,000 per order. This made him another $750,000.

"There's still more. Many of the customers continued ordering coins and collections from him for some time, creating extra income every year. All of this from an original promotion that began with a $19-dollar offer."

According to Ken, the secret is this: "Never look at customers in terms of one-time sales. Go back to them for repeat business. In sales, "It is what comes after the original sale that matters most."

Power Point

"It is what comes after the original sale that matters most."

–Ken Kerr

Ken also shared the following statistics regarding repeat sales:

• Years ago, Home Depot found that its typical customer spent an average of $38 per sale. However, based upon a lifetime of repeat sales with the same customer, the total amount per customer could soar to $25,000.

• Continental Airlines discovered that the long-term economic value of a customer standing before a ticket agent could be as much as one hundred times the amount of that day's ticket transaction. Tom Peters, one of America's top success authorities, also teaches salespeople this concept. He tells them to "consider every customer to be a potential lifelong relationship, generating word-of-mouth references as well as future business."[1]

Power Point Question

Do you have additional products and/or services you could offer your new and/or existing customers?

"Other seed fell on good soil, where it produced a crop – a
hundred, sixty or thirty times what was sown."
—Matthew 13:8 (NIV)

$\mathbf{M}$oney and fame cannot prevent a person from feeling lonely. Even being around other people is not a guaranteed cure-all. Feelings of isolation and detachment can strike even in the middle of a crowd.

A feeling of loneliness not only affects a person's attitude, relationships, and outlook on life, but it can also affect their physical health. A report issued by The National Institute of Health stated, "The most predictive risk factor for heart disease is loneliness."[1]

Catherine Marshall knows how painful and disabling this feeling can be. Before becoming a best-selling author, she experienced a heartrending bout with loneliness as a result of her husband's untimely death. She describes it in this way: "During busy hours I could forget the pain of loneliness. Then some tiny thing...brought it all flooding back."[2]

I personally had to battle loneliness and a feeling of isolation after the untimely death of my first wife, Cindy. If you—or a friend—are feeling detached, sad, or lonely, here are some strategies to beat back loneliness.

STRATEGIES TO BEAT BACK LONELINESS

1. DEVELOP NEW DREAMS: Dreams give hope and bring a fresh spark to life. I remember a quote from an elderly triathlon runner who said, "No one is ever alone who has a dream."

2. GET IN MOTION: Find new things to achieve or get involved in. Don't fritter away your time; create, get involved in a project, do something.

3. CONTACT FRIENDS: Make a list of your loved ones, friends, and acquaintances. Make it a point to contact them regularly.

4. HELP OTHERS: No matter where you live or what your interests or skills may be, there are people who need your help. Show interest in their lives. It will bring joy to yours.

5. TAKE CARE OF YOUR HEALTH: Improper diet, low blood sugar, or other health issues can magnify negative feelings. Watch your diet and exercise regularly.

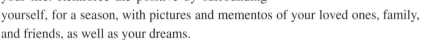

Power Point

"No troubles that life can bring need cast us adrift."[4]

–Catherine Marshall

6. REST: Recharge your body. Tired people tend to respond negatively to situations. Rested people can normally cope better—emotionally and physically.

7. COUNT RIGHT: Focus on the good things that have happened and are happening in your life. Reinforce the positive by surrounding yourself, for a season, with pictures and mementos of your loved ones, family, and friends, as well as your dreams.

8. REMEMBER GOD: You are never really alone because God loves you. He is as near as your prayers. Catherine believes that this is the most important key. "Loneliness is a real wound—a gaping hole in the human spirit. It is God alone who can finally heal the brokenhearted."[3]

If you are dealing with grief or loneliness, I recommend that you begin to activate these strategies. In the words of William Faulkner: "Anyone who removes a mountain begins by carrying away small stones."

Power Point Question

Do you or someone you know need to implement the above strategies?

———————

"He delivered them out of their distresses."
—Psalm 107:6

News Headline

EXTRA!
EXTRA!

Final Edition

Star Has Deathbed Regrets

It was reported that the 67-year-old star, who died in the arms of his fourth wife, was racked with shame and guilt as he apologized for the reckless way he had lived his life. He was deeply hurt that his three children from previous marriages refused to visit him on his deathbed.

How do you want to be remembered?

This is an important question to ask yourself when approaching the sunset days of your life. However, it is also something to ponder when ending almost any activity. Stephen Covey, *New York Times* best-selling author, believes that it helps people's inner guidance systems if they take time to contemplate how they want to be remembered when something ends.

In reference to one's life he states, "At your memorial service what would you desire each of the speakers to say about you and the life you have lived? What characteristics would you want them to share about that they have seen in you that impressed them? What contributions and achievements would you want them to remember?"[1]

Some might talk about your career successes while others share personal stories that were meaningful to them. Family members would probably reveal shared times together, plus characteristics that were important in their development. Of these characteristics, I believe that one of the most important things to be remembered for is a life marked by exemplary character. Living with integrity creates a good path for others to follow, especially one's own children.

Such was the life of my father, Dr. Irvine Harrison.

Dad was a decisive leader who had the ability to persevere and win. Besides being immensely successful, having earned two doctorate degrees, serving as the president of a college, and enjoying achievements in many different arenas, my father lived a life based upon principles. Dad was a man of wisdom, love, forgiveness, and integrity. He did not just read the Bible, but he also did his best to live it.

As I stood overlooking his casket at the memorial service attended by hundreds gathered there from across the nation, I was so grateful to be the son of a man who had positively influenced the lives of so many people. That day my eulogy contained a reference to my dad's characther.

WHAT DO I TELL YOU ABOUT DAD AFTER HE IS GONE?

Do I tell you about my feelings for my father?

That I loved him and respected him, that I will miss him?

Do I tell you about our great family experiences?

How he invested in his children by including them in many trips and outings?

Do I tell you about his concern for his son's future?

How he gave caring advice and financial support for my education and career?

Do I tell you about his life of character and integrity?

That I never heard him tell a lie nor saw him cheat anyone?

I believe that one of the most important things that a father can leave behind are not money and inheritances, but rather positive memories and an exemplary life example.

My dad died on my 29th birthday. For my present that year, I received an incredible heritage: a memory of a man of stability who loved his family, had faith in God, and daily lived a life of character. These memories and his life's example continue to inspire and guide me throughout my life.

Power Point Question

What do you want to be remembered for?"

"The just man…his children are blessed after him."
—Proverbs 20:7

News Headline

Final Edition

EXTRA! EXTRA!

Student Honesty Linked To Discounts

University students offered a discount card good at local shops if they sign a pledge not to cheat.

Honesty did not give my friend George Reece discounts at stores. However, it did provide him to opportunity to become a partner in a development firm.

As a young carpenter, George started his career building homes. He operated his own construction business for several years. Then a large home-building firm noticed his superior work ethic and the quality of his projects. They hired him to become one of their foremen. Because he was faithful, hardworking, and performed well, he received several promotions.

One day, the two senior partners of the company asked George to meet with them. As they were sitting in a secluded area of a restaurant, they started asking him questions about his work and job. Finally, one of them leaned forward and asked, "George, if it was necessary, for the good of the company, would you lie for us?"

George's thoughts raced: *If I don't answer correctly, there goes my opportunity with this firm.* He pondered. *Would he be willing to lie for them?* He knew that answering yes might be the only way to keep his job and get the promotion he desired.

THE VALUE OF INTEGRITY

After a brief pause, George took courage and confidently stated, "I'm sorry, but I could not lie for you." The senior partner leaned back, gave a sigh of relief, and said, "That is the right answer because we know that if you won't lie for us then you won't lie to us. We want to offer you a position as a partner in the firm."

For George, that one decision not to compromise his integrity opened up a whole new dimension of living for him. As Managing Partner of a development company that does over $200 million of income a year, he travels on a private jet. He is enjoying life with his wife and family, has three homes, and is a generous giver to his church and charities. All this happened because he made being honest a foundational strategy of his life.

Power Point

"Honesty is the single most important factor having a direct bearing on...success."[2]

–Ed McMahon

William F. James, founder of Boys Town of Missouri, said, "There are really only three things necessary for success: first, normal intelligence; second, determination; and third, absolute honesty. One cannot be a little dishonest—it is all the way or nothing."[1]

John Wooden, the most successful collegiate basketball coach of all time, taught, "Talent can get you to the top but only character can keep you there."

Power Point Question

How would you have responded to the question about lying?

—————————

"They that deal truly are [the Lord's] delight."
—Proverbs 12:22

News Headline

Final Edition

EXTRA! EXTRA!

Sheriff Is Resident Of Jail He Built

A law officer is in jail after pleading no contest to six felony counts for filing false travel claims.

When he was in office, the sheriff fought for years to build a new jail for the county. Now, he has become a resident of that jail.

It is one thing to be in jail because you committed a crime. However, what is you were in jail and did not need to be?

Author Lou Tice, president of The Pacific Institute in Seattle, Washington, shares such an incident in his book *Smart Talk*. "Imagine yourself imprisoned. Then someone comes along and tells you, 'You imprisoned yourself. You chose to be your own judge and jury. You sentenced yourself to a life of poverty, or mediocrity, or to being an ineffective person. You do not need to stay in jail. The key to the cell door is in your pocket. You can unlock it and walk out free.'"[1]

Tice is referring to people who are imprisoned by their thinking, people who believe that their current reality is fixed. A person's beliefs can literally determine the limitations that they accept and lives with.

Best-selling author Suze Orman refers to this limiting mind-set, stating, "The road to financial freedom begins not in a bank or even in your financial planner's office. It begins in your head—your thoughts."[2]

Several years ago, Tim Flynn, one of my closest friends, made a decision to "unlock" his limiting beliefs and experience a whole new life. When I challenged Tim to plan a "mental breakout," he was making just $15,000 per year. Soon thereafter, he personally made $3.5 million – in one day. Now he operates several businesses, is positively impacting our generation, and is mentoring others on how to enjoy all that God intends for them.

Here are some of Tim Flynn's success strategies:

1. PRIORITIZE: 20 percent of your work will produce 80 percent of the results. Do more of the 20 percent.

2. INTEGRITY: Require yourself and your staff to operate at the highest level of honesty and integrity.

3. QUALITY: Reputation, based upon how you perform your jobs, is one of your best forms of advertising.

4. FRIENDSHIP: Surround yourself with people of excellence and character.

5. TIMING: Learn to "read" the rhythms of your customers and the marketplace.

Power Point

"**True success is... the ability...to sustain.**"
—Tim Flynn

6. THINK LONG-TERM: True success is not the ability to obtain, but to sustain.

7. HELP OTHERS: God gave you a past so that you could help give others a future.

If you feel trapped by limiting beliefs, stop making excuses and organize a "breakout." As Tim says, "While losers are trying to explain the waves in the storm that sunk them, champions are building a new ship."

Power Point Question

Do you have limiting beliefs that are holding you captive?

_____

"A wise man will hear, and will increase learning."
—Proverbs 1:5

Reading the article about former president George H. W. Bush parachuting onto the grounds of his presidential library on his birthday reminded me of a time some friends and I had with him at a luncheon in Tampa, Florida. During our time together, he was asked what he perceived to be the most difficult problem facing the United States today. Bush replied, "The most serious problem facing America is the decline of the traditional family."

I personally believe that one of the things that have caused this decline is that so many couples get too busy. Figuratively, they only parachute into their each other's lives for meals, social events, and occasional romance. Over time, the closeness and intimacy that they once shared fades away like paint on a sun-scorched building.

Yet, when most achievers come to the sunset years of their lives, it is not their careers but rather their spouses and children that matter most to them. For instance, famous explorer, Admiral Richard Byrd wrote on his death bed, "At the end of life the only thing that really matters is family. Anything and everything else is insubstantial."[1]

Billy Graham once said, "I made a big mistake. I left my family too much. If I could do it again I would spend more time with them."[2]

Zig Ziglar believes that the secret to longevity of marriage is this: "Believe that love and romance will be alive as long as the marriage exists—and that the marriage will exist as long as you do."[3] Former president Jimmy Carter concurs, "My first loyalty is and will always be family."[4]

Best-selling author Gary Smalley believes that the main ingredient for a loving and lasting marriage is honor. He states, "Honor basically means to attach a high value, worth, or importance to a person. If your spouse feels less important than your vocation or activities, then you are not honoring him or her as the most important person in your life. My wife is worth more to me than anything on this earth… and she knows it."[5]

Arvella Schuler believes that this mindset is a key to the strength and happiness of her marriage to Dr. Robert Schuller: "Our slogan is that together we are a great team."[6]

Power Point

"**The most serious problem facing America is the decline of the traditional family.**"

–George H. W. Bush

Great marriages and families don't just happen. It takes commitment, understanding, and patience. However, the benefits are well worth the effort.

If you are not experiencing the relationship that you desire, do what best-selling author Randy Gibbs recommends: "Decide what each of you must be and do in order to have what you want."[7]

Power Point Question

How can you improve your relationship with your spouse?

"Submitting yourselves one to another."
—Ephesians 5:21

News Headline

Final Edition

EXTRA!
EXTRA!

Arab Sheik Buys 40 College Degrees

A rich oil baron who cannot read or write has received more than 40 college degrees, six of them doctorates.

The receiving of college diplomas, medals, awards, or citations is very important to some people. Not only do such honors furnish an element of personal pride and recognition, but they also often cause a future increase in income in the marketplace.

Because of the power and prestige that is attached to earning money or being honored with degrees and awards, people will often put forth extraordinary effort to receive them. This sheik got his degrees from a university in his hometown—that he built. Since one of my daughters, Wendy Joy Murakami, did not own a university, she had to be more creative to receive an award that she greatly desired.

Wendy has always been a determined, bright, and innovative person. At university, she was able to maintain academic excellence even though she traveled with me to several overseas meetings and assisted at many of my Increase Events.

For her senior project, she led a team that did a masterful job of analyzing a local business and coming up with creative ways to increase its sales and profits. In fact, the report of the results of their project was so good that it was declared the best senior paper by the school of business. The university even submitted it for state competition.

Wendy was ecstatic about this honor, which showcased her superior marketing and management skills. Then she discovered that no formal recognition or award was given by the school of business for having the best senior project. Since the school gave recognition to other academic accomplishments, and since this project was such a major undertaking, she could not understand why it was not treated similarly.

THE REWARDS OF INNOVATION AND DETERMINATION

Instead of accepting this "non-recognition status quo," she began the process of trying to get the recognition for the team she believed the task merited. She talked to her teacher and the department chairman and pushed through the various academic channels until an idea was born. She prepared a proposal for the business school to offer a Best Senior Paper Award to be presented each year as part of the award presentations that take place during the hooding ceremonies on graduation weekend. She even sent along a sample award that she had prepared on her computer.

Power Point

"When a powerful hunger for your dreams is driving you...the ideas will come."[1]

–Les Brown

The dean responded, "It's never been done before, but why not?"

A few weeks later, on graduation weekend, our family attended the hooding ceremony. Several students received academic and merit awards. Many parents radiated with pride at the accomplishments of their offspring. However, none could have been any prouder than I was. My daughter not only received an award, but she had the innovativeness and determination to create the award—for her team, herself, and all those recipients who would come after them in the future.

Power Point Question

What has it cost you not to pursue harder what you know to be worthwhile goals and dreams?

"I pursue what is good."
—Psalm 38:20 (NIV)

News Headline

Jet Crashes Short Of Runway

EXTRA! EXTRA!

Final Edition

Shortly before the airline crashed, the pilot sent out an urgent message: "Mayday! Mayday! We're going down!"

As the airliner approached the airport, the crew had been concentrated on solving a landing gear problem and had failed to notice the severity of a different developing problem: The plane was running out of fuel. The plane crashed and 174 of the passengers miraculously survived.

This is not an isolated example. According to *USA Today*, over one nine-year period, 39 passenger planes left the gate or took off without enough fuel.[1]

Running out of fuel is a problem that many achievers also face. They start on their flight to success only to discover that they don't have sufficient "fuel" to finish the course. Suddenly they drop out of sight.

During a seminar in Little Rock, Arkansas, I was visiting backstage with Tom Hopkins, one of the world's top sales trainers. He made a profound statement concerning success: "The single most important ingredient to success is the ability to last."

Shortly thereafter, I was talking with a friend who had just spent time with one of the world's premier religious leaders. My friend asked the minister what, more than anything else, was his secret to his achieving such great long-term success. The leader replied, "I lasted."

If you desire to achieve continuing success, it is critical that you have enough energy, resources, and motivation to finish the course.

THE FUELING EDGE

There are several things that you can do to stay "fueled up."

1. MAKE A DREAM LIST: List ten things that you want to achieve, have, and/or give. Regularly envision and talk about these items so that you can "touch" them.

2. ASSOCIATE WITH SUCCESSFUL PEOPLE: Pick up their attitudes and habits. Discover their success secrets. Learn to feel comfortable in their environment.

Power Point

"The single most important ingredient to success is the ability to last."
–*Tom Hopkins*

3. LISTEN TO MOTIVATIONAL AND TEACHING CDs/TAPES: Repetition is the best way to get new truths embedded into your subconscious.

4. MAKE POSITIVE CONFIRMATIONS: Your world is framed by your words. Talk about your desired destinations.

5. READ MIND-EXPANDING BOOKS: Empower and motivate yourself. Learn how others activate success strategies.

6. TAKE TIME FOR ENJOYMENT: Balance work and leisure. See time away from work as a season of refreshing and empowerment. Schedule good times—whether it is engaging in a hobby, driving a "fun" car, or visiting a favorite site.

7. IDENTIFY POSSIBLE FUEL LEAKS: Discover and then either reduce or eliminate those things that drain you of productive energy and creativity.

8. SUSTAIN SPIRITUAL STRENGTH: Through regular devotions, meditation, and prayer, keep your "inner man" strong.

As author Herbert Freudenberger states in his book *Burn Out*, "The more well rounded out your life is, the more protected you are against burn out."[2]

Power Point Question

What are you doing to maintain your "fueling edge"?

"Let us run with patience the race that is set before us."
—Hebrews 12:1

As foolish as it may seem for this lady to have married someone she hardly knew, it is not uncommon for a variation of this scenario to transpire in the marketplace. It occurs when people who do not know each other well come together for a project or large financial transaction. As in the above story, the outcome of the relationship is often disastrous.

James Guinn, who is a CPA, noted author, and seminar speaker form Dallas, Texas, cautions people particularly concerning their investments. Jim's firm specializes in advising major ministries and charities. I have visited with him at numerous board meetings and have had the opportunity to glean from his many years of experience.

The following are some of his warnings of possible risky investments, along with my commentary on them.[1]

DON'T BE THE NEXT VICTIM

1. SOUNDS TOO GOOD: "If the investment sounds unbelievable or unreal, then it probably is." Safe investments seldom offer exorbitant rates of return. A projected high return on an investment causes me to investigate more thoroughly.

2. MUST BE KEPT CONFIDENTIAL: "If, because of the secretive nature of the investment, the promoter discourages you from talking to your financial advisor, CPA, or attorney, be cautious." Most of the millionaires that I know never get involved in any major financial transaction without seeking counsel and advice from trusted aides and advisors.

3. HAS NO TRACK RECORD: "Always insist on receiving verifiable references from associates and/or previous investors. If these are not available, then it is probably best that you don't invest." Even if the person is of good character, he might not have the experience to prudently handle your money. As my friend Myles Munroe says, "Do not trust a person without a history."[2]

4. REQUIRES CASH BEFORE DISCLOSURE: "If the promoter requires cash before furnishing you all the details, be very cautious." Get all the information that you desire or do not hand over the cash that the promoter wants.

Power Point

"Sometimes even when the numbers look right the decision is still wrong."[4]
–Ken Blanchard

5. IT'S NOW OR NEVER: "If the promoter tries to rush you to invest because the investment opportunity is limited and 'going fast,' be very careful." I have personally always made it a policy that I would rather miss a potentially good opportunity than make a big mistake.

When considering major investments, the most important strategy is this: Be cautious and wise. As noted speaker Marilyn Hickey says, "You can have a lot of money, but if you don't have wisdom, you can kiss the money goodbye."[3]

Power Point Question

What strategies do you have in place to prevent yourself from making bad investments?

"A malicious man disguises himself with his lips."
—Proverbs 26:24 (NIV)

News Headline

Final Edition

EXTRA! EXTRA!

Bird Causes Power Outage At Airport

Los Angeles International airport suffered a power outage when a bird landed on a power line causing a blackout and delaying flights for 1-1/2 hours.

Dennis Byrd experienced a "power outage," but it was caused by a collision with a teammate in a football game. The New York Jets defensive end lay flat on his back on the artificial surface of Giants Stadium. All he needed to do was push himself up off the grass, as he had done a thousand times before, and get up. When he tried to move, however, he felt something give way. He heard it, too—a grinding and crunching at the top of his spine. He did not have the power to move his legs. Ten minutes later, he was carted off the field, put into an ambulance, and rushed to the hospital.[1]

Later, it was determined that the collision had broken his neck and left him paralyzed from the waist down.

During the next few months, Dennis had to fight physically, mentally, and spiritually, believing that he would walk again. Dennis' body functions began to improve at what the medical staff told him was an amazing rate. His muscular strength and control got better every day. Soon, he could walk without even limping, bench over 100 pounds, and lift 250 pounds on the leg sled.

In his book *Rise and Walk*, Dennis shared what he believed were the three main forces that enabled him to overcome this tragedy.

WINNING AGAINST ADVERSITY

1. DETERMINATION: "I used determination every minute that I was in the hospital and rehab rooms…Never give up is a lesson that I had learned on the football field."

Jack Canfield, coauthor of the best-selling book *Chicken Soup for the Soul,* believes that having the right attitude is a key to winning in any area of life. He states, "Attitude has a lot to do with a person's success and their ability to get what they want."[2]

2. LOVE OF FAMILY: Dennis shares, "My wife and children were beside me encouraging me when it counted most."

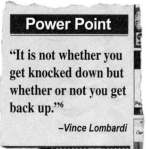

According to best-selling author and authority on successful marriages, Gary Smalley, "Genuine love is far more than feeling. It means a commitment to care for and love your spouse unconditionally...no matter what happens."[3]

3. FAITH IN GOD: Dennis stated, "Knowing that God is with us even when we are down can help to make us whole. I had an awareness of the presence of God undergirding me and giving me the power to bounce back."[4]

A survey of doctors by the American Academy of Family Physicians found that "99 percent of the doctors believe there is an important relationship between spirit and flesh."[5]

Although his football-playing days are now over, Dennis is living a vibrant and happy life sharing with people that they can overcome and win against any adversity.

Power Point Question

If you could hear God whispering to you, "I am with you," would you give up?

"I will never leave you nor forsake you."
—Joshua 1:5 (NIV)

News Headline

Man Trapped In Outhouse Overnight

A man was rescued after spending a hot summer night trapped in an outhouse.

This man's dilemma occurred when the structure's wooden door handle accidentally dropped, trapping him inside. According to authorities, he "was unhurt but in a pretty foul mood."

While we are on the subject of toilets, here is an interesting tidbit: Pioneering heart transplant surgeon Dr. Christian Bernard claimed that the greatest progress in health care in the last five hundred years came not from a drug or surgical procedure, but from the invention of the flushing toilet. The reason is that it provided a means to get rid of waste and thus eliminated many of the plagues that were caused by contaminated water supplies.[1]

The ability to get rid of waste effectively is a key to success in any arena of life. For the achiever, this is particularly true when dealing with time.

Benjamin Franklin once said, "To love life is to love time, because time is the stuff of that is made out of."[2]

Time management expert Edwin Feldman stated, "Just as there are ways to get things done, there are also ways to not get things done. You can serve the clock…or you can put time to work for you."[3]

George Shinn has learned how to effectively use time, and it is one of the key reasons for his great success. Shinn is the owner of the NBA basketball team the New Orleans Hornets and operates some thirty other corporations. He believes that "time is a person's most precious commodity."

Shinn says, "The way you occupy your time should be of paramount importance to you. Whatever your goals are, they must be accomplished in the time you have available. Since time is so valuable in achieving your goals, you should discover what robs you of productive time."[4]

Here are some of my suggestions for how to eliminate time wasters.

HOW TO ELIMINATE TIME WASTERS

1. THE LUNCH HOUR: Considering travel and waiting time, a one-hour lunch appointment can easily use up two to three hours of your time. Consider alternatives, such as meeting on the way to/from work for coffee or breakfast or dining in.

Power Point

"Discover what robs you of productive time."

–George Shinn

2. COMMITTEE MEETINGS: Few activities can waste more time than meetings. Make sure they start on time, end on time, have a definite agenda, and that everyone comes prepared. Maybe even consider having some meetings with everyone standing up.

3. INTERRUPTIONS: When someone walks in to see you, if you are busy, stand up. Your position will automatically reduce the length of the conversation. Carve out of your schedule quality time for creativity.

4. DRIVE TIME: Make your drive time productive by using it to return phone calls (if you are a passenger or can use a phone headset) or listen to teaching/motivational CDs or praise music.

5. IMPROVE YOUR DELEGATING SKILLS: Release activities that can effectively be done by someone else.

Shinn believes that "with forethought and action, you can make your time pay high dividends."[5]

Power Point Question

Which time-wasting activities can you eliminate or drastically reduce?

———————

"It would not be right for us to neglect the ministry of
the word of God in order to wait on tables."
—Acts 6:2 (NIV)

Reading this article about not needing change for vending machines reminded me of an interesting story I came across years ago. It was about an event that happened to a college vice president who was traveling in South Carolina.

One night, after settling into his motel room, the executive walked down the corridor to where the vending machines were located. He stood looking at a machine trying to decide which item to select.

Just then, a ten-year-old boy walked up, stood beside him, and began to poke quarters into the machine. The boy dropped in three, four, six, eight, ten quarters.

Finally, the executive tapped the boy on the shoulder and said, "Son, son, stop. You're putting way too much money in that machine."

The boy turned to him and proudly said, "Oh no, sir. See, the more money I put in, the more stuff I get out."

A POWERFUL INCREASE PRINCIPLE

This little boy identified one of the key reasons why many achievers do not experience increase in certain areas of their lives: They are not making enough deposits.

Personally, I began to experience increased alertness, better stamina, and improved health when I made the decision to increase my deposits of time spent lifting weights and swimming. In the financial arena, when I increased my donations to church and charities, unexpected blessings and unusual business deals were manifested.

The closeness that I enjoy with my children and grandchildren is largely the result of liberal deposits of time in travel, communication, and training.

My spiritual life took on new power and vibrancy when I increased my spiritual deposits. I scheduled regular times of Bible reading, praying, and listening to scripture-based teaching tapes. Now this mind-set governs how I approach most anything in life. Instead of focusing on what I can get, I concentrate on what I can deposit.

Power Point

"The more stuff I put in, the more I get out."

–Boy at vending machine

Are you standing next to the vending machine of life wondering why you are not receiving a greater quantity of health, happiness, spiritual endowment, and/or financial rewards? If so, I would suggest that you consider increasing your deposits.

In the words of my friend the late Dr. Lester Sumrall, "A person cannot grab their way to success. They release their way to success."

Power Point Question

How might an increase in deposits of time, money, or prayer benefit you?

_____

"The generous soul will be made rich."
—Proverbs 11:25 (NKJV)

News Headline

Final Edition

EXTRA! EXTRA!

Fuss Over Backward Cap

School administrators banned an alumnus from school grounds for six months because he wore a Texas Rangers baseball cap backward.

Because officials considered a backward cap to be possible gang attire, the man had a problem. To overcome the situation with the cap, all he had to do was turn it around.

Likewise, in life, sometimes all we need to do to change a problem into an opportunity is to "turn it around." This is what one of my sons-in-law, Tim Redmond, had to do recently.

Years ago, Tim played a key role in starting up a computer software company. Under Tim's direction, the business went from four to over four hundred employees. Because of its success, a major national corporation paid millions of dollars to purchase the company and its customer base.

Tim took a portion of his proceeds from the sale and made some long-term investments. He then decided to form a seminar company for the purpose of introducing Bible-based success strategies to audiences around the world.

Because of contacts that he had in Bolivia, he chose to do his first international seminar in the capital city of Santa Cruz. Committing over $25,000 for the program budget, he asked me to join him as a featured speaker. Attendance was expected to be around five hundred people.

Tim contracted with some local people to handle publicity and ticket sales. Ten days before the seminar date, Tim flew to Bolivia for a pre-event inspection trip. He discovered a situation that was disastrous. Although there appeared to be great interest in the seminar, only eighteen people had actually purchased tickets.

TURNING AROUND A "BACKWARD" SITUATION

At this point, most people would probably have cancelled the seminar and taken their losses, but not Tim. Instead, he rolled up his sleeves and, with a fresh determination, sprang into action.

First he went to the national newspaper and negotiated a trade—ad space in the paper in exchange for staff training and free tickets to the seminar. Then he created a group discount program and personally started contacting many local businesses, heralding the benefits of their employees attending the seminar. When I arrived a week later, he had arranged for me to be driven straight to a television station to share on a national talk show.

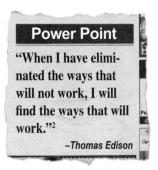

Power Point

"When I have eliminated the ways that will not work, I will find the ways that will work."[2]

–Thomas Edison

By the morning of the seminar, everyone was amazed at the turnaround. In ten days' time, the numbers had skyrocketed from eighteen to over six hundred.

All this happened because one person of vision would not accept it when things were "backward." Instead, he believed enough in himself—and his God—to turn the circumstances around. As Tim says, "Don't be captivated by the height of the mountain rather than your ability to climb."[1]

Power Point Question

What is your instinctive response to negative situations —flight or fight?

"For the battle is the Lord's,
and he will give you into our hands."
—1 Samuel 17:47

News Headline

Final Edition

EXTRA! EXTRA!

Healthy Habits Reduce Heart Disease

Studies show that small changes in lifestyle patterns and eating habits can greatly reduce the risk of heart disease.

Y ou've heard it before: For better health, eat right and exercise. Millions of people suffer unnecessarily with poor health and die prematurely because they have unhealthy lifestyles, are not eating a proper diet, and are not exercising.

For instance, researchers at the American Heart Association's annual meeting in Atlanta reported that there is more evidence than ever that simple good habits can reduce the risk of heart disease.[1]

My friend Dr. Patrick Quillin, who is one of America's foremost nutritionists, health lecturers, and broadcasters, also agrees. He states, "Through years of neglect many people turn their bodies that are built for activity into bodies that can barely get off the couch. Then when their malnourished and poorly maintained bodies begin to break down, they use drugs to subdue the symptoms of the illness, rather than dealing with the underlying cause of the disease."[2]

Dr. Quillin believes that people's lives can change when they come to the realization that "God's purpose of providing food is to nourish the body with essential nutrients found in plants and animals." He states, "You cannot enjoy life as God intended nor accomplish your 'mission' if your body wears out too soon."[3]

From a lecture at one of my Increase Events, here are some of Dr. Quillin's ABCs of better health.

ABCs OF BETTER HEALTH

A. ANTIOXIDANTS: Curtail aging and prevent disease by eating plenty of fresh whole fruits and vegetables.

B. BACK MAINTENANCE: The spinal cord is an extension of the brain. Keep it aligned and strong.

C. CHEW FOOD THOROUGHLY: When food is swallowed too quickly, it cannot be absorbed into the body.

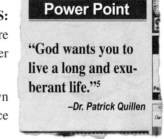

D. DRINK FLUIDS BETWEEN MEALS: Drink minimal amounts of fluids while you are eating. They dilute digestive juices. Drink water between meals.

> **Power Point**
>
> **"God wants you to live a long and exuberant life."**[5]
>
> *–Dr. Patrick Quillen*

E. E VITAMIN: Several studies have shown that taking vitamin E on a regular basis can reduce the risk of heart attacks.

F. FAT REDUCTION: A high-fat diet brings many health hazards, such as clogging of the arteries and acceleration of the aging process

G. GREEN FOODS: Eat lots of vegetables, some of which should be uncooked. Buy organic produce when possible.

Dr. Chris Enriquez, who operates a famous wellness clinic in Ft. Lauderdale, Florida, concurs, "Instead of the traditional reactive approach to health that is so common, I suggest a proactive approach. In other words, I advocate seeking to maintain good health instead of simply reacting whenever bad health comes along."[4]

According to Dr. Quillin, we must either take time for wellness or we will be forced to take time for illness.

Power Point Question

What are you doing nutritionally to improve your health?

_____

"Eat what is good and delight yourself with rich nourishment."
—Isaiah 55:2 (author's paraphrase)

News Headline

Final Edition

EXTRA! EXTRA!

Woman Trapped By Pig

A huge pig, the size of a Shetland pony, trapped a terrified woman in her home. Australian Rangers finally rescued the lady but the massive animal escaped.

Many stories have been written about people who become trapped by storms or accidents and had to be rescued. It is common to trap animals by fairly unusual for people to become trapped by them.

However, what is very common but not always recognized, is that people can be trapped by their emotions. So says Dr. Don Colbert, one of America's foremost anti-aging doctors. Dr. Colbert has written numerous best-selling health related books and is regularly seen on national television programs.

One of his books is titled *Deadly Emotions.* In it he provides examples and evidences on the relationship between stress/emotional hurts and physical problems. When I read this book I was so impressed with what he wrote that I scheduled him to be a featured speaker at one of my Increase Events. Since then, he has returned and shared on numerous occasions.

At one of those Events, Dr. Colbert discussed this issue of how past hurts can harm one's health. He stated, "Emotions are meant to be expressed and felt. However, oftentimes when someone gets emotionally hurt, they internalize their feelings. Over time these negative feelings escalate and become a seething mix of anger and hostility. The trapped emotions then seek expression." He went on to state:

"When we bury negative emotions we are burying something that is living."

Dr. Colbert explained that these trapped emotions normally cause one of two things to occur, if not both. First, the person begins having problems containing their anger. As a result, negative verbal outbursts become common. Most of the time the person is not aware of the cause of their damaging and hurtful behavior. They simply find themselves living "tensed and ready to fight back."

The other primary way that trapped negative feelings manifest themselves is that the person begins to experience numerous health issues. This happens because when one represses anger and fear, the tension is turned inward. The body transfers this tension to different muscle groups. Then one day that individual awakens with a stiff back, a painful neck, digestion problems, or finds that some organ is malfunctioning.

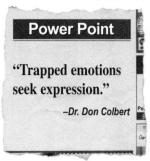

Power Point

"**Trapped emotions seek expression.**"

–Dr. Don Colbert

The good news is that one can do a great deal to pull the plug on the toxic emotions that fuel deadly and painful diseases, plus damage relationships.

If you, or someone you know, is suffering from repressed anger or intense negative emotions, Dr. Colbert recommends the following:

1. Identify any past hurtful events that might be causing current negative physical and/or emotional problems. Deal with them as needed through counseling and/or prayer.

2. When you feel tension building from within, take "time-outs." Separate yourself, even if only briefly, from the irritation.

3. Learn to relax. Practice deep-breathing exercises in order to decompress.

4. Apologize to others quickly. Don't let negative emotions grow inside of you or others.

5. Ask God to forgive you when your outbursts hurt others. Also ask forgiveness of any whom you might have wounded with your unkind words.

Dr. Colbert believes that one of the best ways to deal with past negative experiences is to choose to instead think about those things and events that evoke positive emotions within you. He says, "Focus on them. Emphasize them. Reflect often on them. They are your best line of defense against toxic emotions."

Power Point Question

How could you better deal with hurtful events of your past?

"Let not the sun go down upon your wrath."
—Ephesians 4:26

News Headline EXTRA! EXTRA!

Final Edition

Newsboys Band Takes Arena With Them

On tour the group sets up their own inflatable, self-contained air dome.

The Newsboys performed concerts in 65 cities in the United States during their tour. Their air dome is equipped with a million watts of lighting and 150,000 watts of sound, enough to match most any fixed arena in the country.

This group has been popular for over 15 years. They have over 20 number one hits and three gold albums and have sold over three million records.

One of the key reasons that they continue to attract large audiences is that they seek out new and better ways to present their music. While staying consistent in their overall message to music fans of all ages, they periodically reinvent themselves.

UNDERSTANDING YOUR AUDIENCE

In their book, *Shine*, the Newsboys share about the need to keep abreast of one's audience. They believe that the landscape of the world keeps changing. If someone refuses to accept that reality, it causes them to approach the world as they think it should be, rather than as it actually is. The group believes that if we do not learn the way the world thinks and lives we won't be able to address the real needs of people.[1]

The Newsboys are, in effect, using a selling method called "psychographics." Years ago, I effectively employed it when I was a Chrysler dealer in southern California. Psychographics is the study and understanding of various segments of the population and their distinct buying habits based upon their values, attitudes, and lifestyles (VALS). After ascertaining the clients' (audiences') value systems, the sales presentation (message, product, or program offering) can be customized based upon this knowledge.

Frank Bettger, who wrote one of the classic books on sales success, teaches this strategy: "Looking back over my career, the biggest regret that I have is that I did not spend twice as much time studying and servicing my customers' interests."[2]

Business consultant and author Anne Obarski concurs. She believes that once you know the people you are addressing, you can better provide them with attention-getting communication and products.

Obarski teaches that "people like to do business with people who do not take them for granted."[3] She recommends asking yourself four vital questions. These questions can be adapted for any form of interaction, whether it is for sales, everyday conversation, public speaking, or writing.

- Who are your potential customers?
- Where do they live, work, and play?
- What are the demographics of your typical customers?
- What will attract them and/or bring them back to your company?[4]

Once you really know the audience that you are addressing, you will be better able to furnish the products, services, and programs that best satisfy their needs and desires.

Power Point Question

How well do you know the needs and wants of your audience or clients?

"Do to others as you would have them do to you."
— Luke 6:31 (NIV)

Final Edition

EXTRA! EXTRA!

News Headline

A Long Ride To Harvard

A Los Angeles teenager was one of the most unlikely people to be selected to attend Harvard University, let alone to be awarded a "Full-Ride Scholarship."

Donald Trump once said that the #1 key to being a successful business person is determined by how you respond to adversity.

If that statement is correct, then Khadijah Williams has great success ahead of her.

As long as she can remember, Khadijah had to float between shelters and motels and armories. In 12 years time she attended 12 different schools while living out of garbage bags, sometimes among pimps and drug dealers.

When shelters would fill up or money ran out, she and her mother would pack what little they had and board a bus to find housing somewhere else. It was not unusual for Khadijah to have to hunt for her next meal or determine what was a secure place to sleep.

When she was in her junior year of high school, she had to commute from an Orange County armory to school in Los Angeles by riding connecting buses. She awoke at 4:00 a.m. and returned around 11:00 p.m. Yet, in spite of all the challenges, she was able to keep her grade-point average just below a 4.0 (straight A's).

Her secret? At every stop, she pushed herself in each school's gifted student program. She was diligent in her studies, plus she read four to five books a month. In addition, she reached out for assistance from organizations and mentors.

Her reward for all this effort? A full scholarship to Harvard University.

My friend, Dr. Don Colbert likes to compare this "can-do" attitude to Annie in the box-office hit musical by the same name. This curly-topped, redheaded orphan croons her undying optimism: "The sun will come out tomorrow." Despite living in poverty and abandonment, Annie refuses to see her orphan status as permanent. She does not accept helplessness. In fact, her character depicts the exact opposite: hopefulness.

Power Point

"I will use my unwavering will and motivation to pursue."[1]

–Khadijah Williams

There is no promise that life is going to be absent of adversity and challenges. However, our response to these negative seasons will determine whether we will fade off into the memories of a distant past or continue to live a life of meaning and impact.

Power Point Question

How well do you respond to adversity?

"The trouble of the passing hour may result in a solid glory."
—2 Corinthians 4:17

News Headline

EXTRA!
EXTRA!

Final
Edition

Hotels Face Lawsuits On Surcharges

Lawyers are suing corporations that have been billing customers with hidden surcharges for everything from electricity to pool usage.

There are times, such as in the above story, when, in order to settle a grievance, a lawsuit might be necessary. In our society, It is very easy to sue if you believe you have been wronged. However, being the instigator of a lawsuit can have negative consequences such as lost time and money.

For instance, a former Ohio State University football player sued a fellow player for $2 million, claiming that he had punched him. The trail took two weeks. The player spent thousands of dollars for expert witnesses and attorney fees. In the end, he was awarded only $6,000.[1]

Sometimes, the real question to ask is not "Can I?" but rather "Should I?"

TO SUE OR NOT TO SUE

1. ALTERNATE COURSES OF ACTION: Has every other option been examined? Might there be someone, whom both parties respect, who could be a mediator or "communication bridge builder"?

2. OPPOSING PERSPECTIVE: Can you see the issue form the other party's point of view and understand his position and feelings? If he is operating with wrong information and/or wrong beliefs, a meeting or phone call might avoid the cost and time of a suit.

3. CERTAINTY OF OUTCOME: Have you carefully weighed the strengths and legal options of the other side? You could spend a lot of time and money and then end up with an unfavorable outcome. Also, if the other party countersues, you could end up losing more.

4. ATTENTION DEFICIT: What is pursuing the suit going to cost you, your employees and/or your company in lost focus and energy? Could you generate more money by spending the same amount of time on increasing income?

5. EMOTIONAL IMPACT: Will pursuing the suit cause you and/or some of your key people to be consumed for a season with negative issues that could trigger personal anger strife, and hostility? Might this also negatively affect the health, marriages, personal relationships, and/or spiritual power of those involved?

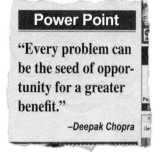

Power Point

"Every problem can be the seed of opportunity for a greater benefit."

–Deepak Chopra

6. COLLECTING ON THE JUDGMENT: If you win a judgment, but the loser either doesn't have any money or assets or has "buried them," what good is the verdict? Might additional time, money, and effort need to be spent attempting to collect?

7. FORGIVENESS: Have you considered making the matter a "seed" for future harvests? Deepak Chopra teaches that "every problem can be the seed of opportunity for a greater benefit."[2] The apostle Paul in the Bible also taught on this principle: "Whatsoever a man soweth, that shall he also reap" (Galatians 6:7).

Before entering into a lawsuit, consider the above points. It could save you a lot of money, headaches, and heartaches.

Power Point Question

Before pursuing a lawsuit, which of the above points should you most consider?

_____

"There is a way that seems right…but in the end it leads to death."
—Proverbs 14:12 (NIV)

I never left my wife behind. However, there was a time when I almost had to fly off and leave my eleven-year-old daughter Michelle behind at one of the world's busiest airports. Instead, we both learned a life lesson that day about the power of spoken words.

"DADDY, I STILL BELIEVE..."

When my children were younger, if I had a weekend engagement that was not a great distance, I would take one of them with me. Little Michelle was so looking forward to her turn to take her next trip and have Daddy all to herself.

When we arrived at our gate at the airport to board for our flight to San Fransisco, I was faced with a dilemma. The plane was oversold. I had a confirmed assigned seat, but the agent said there was no seat for my daughter. Plus, there were fifteen other standby passengers who had higher priority to board.

I quickly went over to the gates of the two other airlines that flew to San Francisco. All their flights were sold out. Then I raced back to my gate and tried begging the agent for a seat for my daughter. He again informed me there were no seats. Furthermore, the agent stated that unless I immediately boarded the flight, he was going to give my seat to someone else.

There seemed to be no way for Michelle to get on the plane. I quickly got down on my knees and told her that there was not a seat. Mommy would have to come get her and take her home. Tears started to roll down her cheeks as she said, "Daddy, I still believe I'll get on that plane."

I tried to think of what words I could say to preserve her precious faith. Just then I noticed, the gate agent frantically waving to me. As I rushed over to him, he whispered, "I have one empty seat. You will not be sitting together, but take your daughter with you on the plane."

Little Michelle quickly and happily boarded the plane and nestled into her first row seat, where she was pampered by the flight attendants the entire flight.

Power Point

"Faith is God's signal to go into action."[1]

–Charles Stanley

After my speaking engagement, we had a wonderful time together in San Francisco riding the cable cars, going to Fisherman's Wharf, and enjoying the sights.

One other thing: When I sat down in my seat, the man next to me exclaimed, "My wife did not get on the plane. She was out at the gate confessing to me, 'There are too many standbys. I will never get on that plane.'"

My daughter's words had created an environment that caused someone to change their mind and give her a seat.

As an achiever, it is critical that you realize that great good and change can take place by speaking faith-filled words into negative situations. Train yourself to speak of desired dreams and results.

Power Point Question

Do the words of your mouth create opportunities?

"Death and life are in the power of the tongue."
—Proverbs 18:21

The Red Kettle fundraising drive, which takes place during the holiday season, raises money to buy toys for needy children and to help the homeless. People were shocked that anyone would steal money intended to help others in need.

Conversely, the lives of my friends Don and Marlene Ostrom were changed when they gave money to—not took money from—a charity.

Don and Marlene are multimillionaires who operate assisted living facilities in the Northwest, employing a staff of hundreds of people. In addition, Don has traveled to over sixty countries, speaking and teaching people to believe in, and act upon, many of the success principles found in the Bible. He recently wrote a great book called *Millionaire in the Pew*.

Several years ago, Don and Marlene were struggling financially. They had opened one of their first nursing homes. It was a huge four-story, 140-bed facility. However, they had a problem. There were too many empty beds, and they couldn't seem to get them occupied. As a result, month after month, the facility was running in the red with expenses exceeding income. Sometimes, they had to borrow from other accounts just to cover payroll for that facility. Knowing that the negative situation could not go on much longer, Don was unsure of what to do to turn things around.

One day, Marlene said to him, "Donald, we should give God a donation from this facility." Don exploded, "How can we give from a business that is in the red? We can't give when we aren't making any money! You just don't understand business."

In spite of his logical reasoning, Marlene still felt strongly that they should make a donation. She prayed about the situation. A few weeks later, Don himself felt impressed to do something.

From the facility's bank account, they made a donation to their church in the amount of one thousand dollars. Don says that "everything changed when we released that money. Almost immediately, the beds began to fill up. Soon, the facility became profitable."[1]

Power Point

"Everything changed when we released that money."

– *Don Ostrom*

Don believes that "the decision to obey God, no matter what the circumstances, established an important core value in my life. It has stayed with me all these years and has brought me exceptional success."[2]

Rabbi Daniel Lapin teaches on the strategy that the Ostroms used to create their financial breakthrough. "How does one go about excavating a money pipeline? Sometimes the only way to get something in is to first dig a route out." He goes on, "Pump money outward from you to the world out there. That action will create conduits that…are able to be used for cash flow in the reverse direction."[3]

As Don says, "God can multiply your obedience many times beyond what you can imagine."

Power Point Question

Might something you release cause you to experience a breakthrough?

"Cast thy bread upon the waters:
for thou shalt find it after many days."
—Ecclesiastes 11:1

News Headline

EXTRA!
EXTRA!

Final
Edition

Thieves Steal Family History

A lifetime of pictures and videos of the family were among some of the items taken from a couple's station wagon as it sat in their driveway.

The pictures were packed in the vehicle for a trip the next morning to a family reunion. They were the family's only pictures of the children growing up.

Every day, thefts and disasters of different kinds and magnitudes unexpectedly occur. Because of this reality, it is important to focus on protecting your valuable keepsakes and proprietary resources.

This is not to encourage the adoption of a mentality that continually expects bad things to happen. However it is always best to be aware of possible negative occurrences and to develop prevention and response strategies. In this way, any negative impact will be minimized if and when a harmful situation occurs.

This type of thinking is one reason why former New York City mayor Rudolph Giuliani and his officials were able to quickly respond to the tragic events of September 11, 2001. Giuliani shares, "Throughout my time as mayor, we conducted tabletop exercises designed to rehearse our response to a wide variety of contingencies…such as an attack."[1]

You probably will never have to deal with a big disaster. However, a smaller crisis, such as fire or theft, is a distinct possibility.

For instance, a minister friend of mine had his briefcase stolen at an airport. In it were his Bible and sermon notes. It took him untold hours to reconstruct the lost information.

Here are some of my suggestions for how to be more disaster resilient.

HOW TO BE DISASTER RESILIENT

1. THINK BACKUP: Back up important documents and computer files regularly. Keep them stored in a safe place off the premises.

2. PROTECT FROM FIRE: Store important pictures, legal documents, and working papers in fireproof cabinets on the premises.

3. PROTECT FROM THEFT: Keep confidential financial and personal material double locked (locked in files in a locked office). Require distinct individual security codes for office entry after hours.

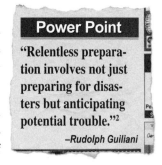

Power Point

"Relentless preparation involves not just preparing for disasters but anticipating potential trouble."[2]

–Rudolph Guiliani

4. PROTECT PRIVACY: Require all employees to sign proprietary rights statements protecting the confidentiality and privacy of customers.

5. ESTABLISH A RECYCLE POLICY: Do not release new confidential information to employees without the old information having been returned.

6. KEEP IT CONFIDENTIAL: Most trash is public domain once it leaves the premises. Place shredding machines in the offices where confidential reports and documents are discarded.

Remember, catastrophic events may be harmful, but they need not be disastrous.

Power Point Question

Have you adequately protected important pictures, documents, lists, records, and assets?

"Guard what has been entrusted to your care."
—1 Timothy 6:20 (NIV)

News Headline
Final Edition   EXTRA! EXTRA!

Mother Battles Gator To Save Son

A twelve-year-old boy who was snorkeling in a river was bitten on the head by the alligator.

Seeing the emergency, the boy's mother reached out and yanked her son from the mouth of the eleven-foot alligator. The ensuing struggle broke the child's leg but saved his life.

In times of emergency, many people somehow receive the courage and ability to do what is seemingly impossible. However, in the normal course of life, if something seems too difficult for them or when they are confronted with what seems impossible, they either don't try to they give up.

Impossibility thinkers are usually passive. They let things happen to them rather than choosing to direct their lives. In addition, new situations frighten them, so they are normally resistant to change.

Author Dr. Robert Anthony teaches that this does not need to be our reaction to difficulties because "impossible situations are really only problems for which we have not immediate solution." He believes that "impossible problems are merely the difference between where you are, and where you can be."[1]

For example, up until the turn of the century, flight was considered impossible. Then one December day in 1903, the Wright brothers succeeded in getting an airplane in the air. Suddenly, what was believed to be impossible was possible. In fact, many of the things that we use on a regular basis, such as electric lights, telephones, microwaves, and personal computers, were all thought to be impossibilities at one time.

CALLED TO DO THE IMPOSSIBLE

Author Cherie Carter-Scott says, "Ordinary people believe only in the possible. On the other hand, extraordinary people think about and visualize what is impossible as being possible. By this process they begin to see those things as possible."[2] This was the mind-set that the great industrialist Henry Ford once stated that he desired in his employees: "I am looking for a lot of men who have an infinite capacity to not know what can't be done."[3]

The late Bill Bright was the founder and president of an international ministry that had a staff of approximately seven thousand people in nearly one hundred countries. He was a man who believed in doing things that seemed to be impossible. In his book *Believing God for the Impossible*, he exhorted his readers, "We are called to do impossible deeds –to live supernatural lives. To live a supernatural lifestyle we must begin to think supernatural thoughts, make supernatural plans, pray for supernatural results, and expect God to work supernaturally in our own lives."[4]

Power Point

"To be a realist, you must believe in miracles."

–David Ben-Gurion

Anthony Robbins concurs: "People can do virtually anything as long as they muster the resources to believe they can and then take effective action. When you tell yourself you can do it, you open up the pathways that will provide you the resources for achievement."[5] Carter-Scott says, "Whether you believe you can do something or you believe you cannot, you are probably right."[6]

Determine today that the word *impossible* is no longer going to be a barrier to your actions and dreams.

Power Point Question

How can you become a better possibility thinker?

"With God all things are possible."
—Matthew 19:26

News Headline

EXTRA! EXTRA!

Final Edition

Dead Woman Sheds A Tear

Doctors were stunned when a woman they thought was dead shed a tear.

Upon seeing the woman's tear, the emergency-room team brought the woman, whose vital signs had ceased, back to life. Afterward, she stated, "God has given me a second chance."

I had an experience in which my wife "came back to life." However, it was not a resurrection of physical life but rather a restoring of life to our marriage.

For thirty-seven years, I was privileged to be married to a wonderful woman. Cindy was a positive, happy, caring, and vivacious person. Until her untimely death in May of 2000, she filled the lives of so many people with joy and love.

Cindy and I married young. To others we appeared to have a wonderful relationship. However, behind the scenes we were dealing with some serious relationship problems. It all came to a head shortly before our tenth anniversary. One day she ran into the bedroom, fell down on the floor, and, with tears streaming down her face, screamed out, "God, what do I do? I don't love him anymore."

I DON'T LOVE HIM ANYMORE

Cindy later commented, "Our crisis was not caused by any one big thing. Bob was always faithful and he provided well for the family. Yet, at that time of his life, he had a negative attitude. He was always criticizing me and others. Plus, he had gotten so busy with business and sports that the kids and I were not getting enough of the attention we needed.

"Because of these things, I began to get negative. Without either of us fully realizing what was happening, my negative attitude caused love to fly out of our home like a bird flying out of its nest ."

That day, while she was on her knees, a Bible verse came to her remembrance. It was Philippians 4:8: "Whatsoever things are of good report;..if there be any praise, think on these things."

CINDY'S GOOD-REPORT LIST

Cindy pulled out a piece of paper and began to activate the two words 'good report.' She wrote down the things she likes about me – the things I was doing right.

She said, "Every morning and every night, I read, confessed, and added to that list. I began to see more good things about him and our marriage. My thinking and attitude began to change. Soon, my feelings and emotions responded. Fresh love sprang forth and our marriage became better than ever before.

"Bob and I would never have had a second chance at love except for my tearful decision to resurrect dead love by choosing to become a person of good report."

Power Point Question

How many things can you itemize on a "good-report list" of your spouse, parents, or key business associates?

"Whatsoever things are of good report..., think on these things."
—Philippians 4:8

News Headline

EXTRA!
EXTRA!

Final
Edition

Cancer Claims Ted Kennedy

Senator Edward M. Kennedy died from a cancerous brain tumor. It was the grim final chapter in a life marked by exhilarating triumph and shattering tragedy.

When I first heard about Senator Kennedy being diagnosed with terminal cancer, I thought about the physical, mental and emotional challenges that lay ahead for him and loved ones during the next season of his life.

The Bible teaches that, "To everything there is a season…a time to plant, and a time to pluck up; a time to weep and a time to laugh; a time to get, and a time to lose." (Ecclesiastes 3)

I believe that the above principle is true: Life is a collection of seasons. However, I have also discovered that many times we do not experience one season followed by another season. Instead, oftentimes we have to deal with two different seasons taking place simultaneously. In other words, during the same time frame we might find ourselves experiencing laughing and weeping… winning and losing…sowing and reaping.

For example, last year I visited some friends of mine in Ohio, Eric and Gina. They were full of joy as they had just found out that she was pregnant with their first child. However, they were also saddened and deeply concerned as the doctors informed her they had discovered that she had cancer. Within a few months of giving birth to a beautiful baby girl, Gina passed away.

A few months later, I experienced another incident of people having to deal with overlapping seasons. My oldest grandson, Matthew Redmond, was graduating from high school with honors. I hosted a graduation party for him at my home. Over one hundred of his friends and relatives gathered as we honored him celebrating this milestone in his life.

In contrast, the next day Matthew and the Redmond family were saddened and emotionally immersed as they participated in the memorial service and burial of his beloved grandfather, Bill Redmond.

OVERLAPPING SEASONS OF LIFE

Best-selling author and mega-church pastor Rick Warren shares about this "overlapping of seasons of life" as follows:

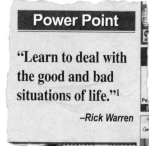

"I used to think that life was hills and valleys—one would go through a dark time and then have a mountaintop experience; that the two went back and forth throughout our lives. I don't believe that anymore.

"I have discovered that rather than life always being a series of hills and valleys or beginnings and endings, many times it's more like two rails on a railroad track: you are experiencing something good and something bad in your life simultaneously.

"For instance, last year has been the greatest year of my life but it has also been the toughest. When my book sold 15 million copies, it made me instantly very wealthy. It also brought a lot of fame that I had never experienced before. On the other hand, we discovered that my wife, Kay, has cancer and the treatment has been very difficult for her. Especially when they are occurring at the same time, one has to learn to deal with the good and the bad situations of life."

If you find yourself dealing with an overlapping season, I would recommend the following: Make a conscious choice to do what is necessary to maintain your emotional equilibrium. Do not ignore the negative situation that you are dealing with but choose to focus on the good things that are happening in your life. Each of life's seasons is full of lessons and experiences that can bring us joy and cause us to be more compassionate, plus bring us closer to God.

Power Point Question

How can you better handle "overlapping seasons?"

"To everything there is a season."
—Ecclesiastes 3:1

News Headline

Final Edition — EXTRA! EXTRA!

New Movie Features 10-minute Segments

In a new twist at moviemaking, fifteen different film directors were given exactly 10 minutes to present their story and vision on screen.

When forced to do so, it was amazing how effective each of those directors made their ten-minute segments.

One of the things that has always amazed me about my wife, Sharon, is how much she can accomplish in a day. Sharon believes that "No one can get more time, but we all can do a better job utilizing the time we have." Sharon is an event planner, musical producer, and seminar teacher. One of the subjects she teaches on is how people can reduce stress while becoming more productive.

One of the strategies for increasing personal productivity is to become more aware of, and better utilize, the numerous 10-minute segments of time that make up each day.

Sharon reminds us that "there are six 10-minute segments in every hour, one hundred forty-four 10-minute segments in every day, and one thousand eight 10-minute segments in every week. The choices we make as to how we value and use each of these 10-minute segments have a lot to do with our personal productivity and happiness in life."

10-MINUTE CHANGES

Sharon illustrates how one can change circumstances in this short period of time: "By spending 10 minutes in quiet meditation, one can totally switch how they react to stress and busyness. Taking a nap for 10 minutes can release fresh energy and cause clearer thinking. Within 10 minutes, a mother can stop what she is doing, bandage her crying toddler's scraped knee, plant a kiss on the their forehead, and be perceived as 'Mother of the Year.' Likewise, a husband can come home after having had an earlier disagreement with his wife, bring her flowers, say the words, 'I'm sorry,' and, within 10 minutes change the course of the whole evening and maybe even their future."

In the spiritual area of life, capturing these short time segments can make a difference. "Spending 10 minutes beginning your day in prayer can bring you joy and make you more peaceable. God can touch your broken spirit and take away your grief or doubt. In time that you can begin to believe that all things are possible. In 10 minutes, you can come forth from a dead situation; spiritual eyes can be opened, and you can get the understanding and creative ideas needed for a turnaround.

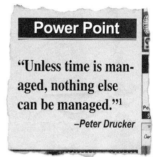

Spending 10 minutes a day reading the Bible can add new power and authority to your life. Additionally, teaching Bible stories and principles to your children or grandchildren for 10 minutes a day can give them a foundation for greater success and a life of purpose."

Of course, Sharon does not believe that everything in one's life will be fixed in 10 minutes. Some things take patience and perseverance. However she does believe that "within 10 minutes, one can receive the wisdom and insight to know what to do and how to fix it."

Sharon says, "If you do not manage your time, it will manage you, so start doing that now—10 minutes at a time."

Power Point Question

How can you better utilize your 10-minute segments of time?

"To everything there is a...time."
—Ecclesiastes 3:1

News Headline — EXTRA! EXTRA!

Final Edition

Chef Fired For Good Cooking

A Swedish cook was fired because his cooking was so good that it was creating lines and causing a shortage of tables.

The restaurant manager told reporters that the cook was terminated because "he was attracting too many people."

This article reminded me of an experience that I had a few years ago in the Palm Springs area of California. Based upon some friends' recommendations, I visited a fast-food restaurant called In-N-Out Burgers for the first time.

The store was located along the interstate adjacent to two other nationally renowned fast-food outlets. As I arrived I was surprised at the difference in the number of cars in the parking lots and drive-thru lines of the three establishments. One restaurant had three vehicles, the next one had six vehicles, and In-N-Out Burgers had thirty-one vehicles. That's right—over 500 percent more vehicles!

I became excited about going inside to discover what would cause this great difference in customer numbers. The restaurant was sparkling clean, but I knew it had to be more than that. The menu offered only six items, so I knew it sure wasn't that. As I sat down and began to eat one of the best hamburgers I have ever enjoyed, I saw the answer. Quality.

Written on my place mat I read the following: "At In-N-Out Burgers, we've always believed that freshness makes a difference you can taste: Our hamburgers are made from fresh, 100 percent pure, locally raised American beef. We make every In-N-Out burger one at a time, cooked fresh to your order. Our buns are baked using old-fashioned sponge dough and contain no preservatives. We don't own a single freezer, microwave, or heat lamp. We make our French fries from real potatoes—fresh each day. Our shakes are still made from real ice cream instead of artificial shake mix." And the list of unique characteristics went on and on.

Success guru and best-selling author Tom Peters believes that "for the successful company, quality cannot just be one more competitive weapon—it must be a consuming passion." He also believes that "quality is perceptual and subjective. It is delivering above expectation. It is having products that contain a 'delight factor'…a startling little touch that makes a customer smile."[1]

Power Point

"Quality…must be a consuming passion."

–Tom Peters

If you don't mind dealing with problems caused by having too many customers or too much income, then take time today to ponder these questions: What are you offering compared to your competition? How can you become the best? The people are out there waiting for you.

Power Point Question

How can you create greater uniqueness for your products and/or services?

"And a great multitude…followed him… when they had heard what great things he did."
—Mark 3:7-8

News Headline

Final Edition

EXTRA! EXTRA!

Prayer Makes A Difference

Ruth Graham is now home and well after teetering on the brink of death for five days.

When her fever, brought on by spinal meningitis, reached 104 degrees, her husband prayed for a miracle. Billy Graham believed that prayer would help his wife, Ruth, to recover. Shortly after he prayed, she sat up in bed, asked the nurses for ice cream, and then pleaded to go home.

Rev. Graham and people in ministry are not alone in the belief that prayer can change natural circumstances. In a survey conducted by the American Academy of Family Physicians, virtually all the doctors questioned believed in a link between the spirit and the health of their patients.[1]

Other recent scientific studies support this view.

In the first known study linking religious faith and prayer to heart patient recovery, a public hospital in San Francisco took four hundred heart patients and divided them into two groups. In the double-blind study, one group was prayed for by strangers who received their names, while the other group was not prayed for. The group that was not prayed for suffered congestive heart failure two and a half times greater than the group that was prayed for.[2]

In another study, Dartmouth Medical School tracked 232 open-heart surgery patients for six months. They found that "the patients who received no strength or comfort from religious faith were over three times (300 percent) more likely to die."[3]

Charles Stanley, renowned author, pastor and national television personality, says, "For a long time the deity of [God] was nothing more to me than Orthodox theology. That is, until I began to think about the fact that God's

Spirit dwells in me."[4] Charles then came to the realization that the presence of God can enable anyone to live a life of greater victory over circumstances.

The late Norman Vincent Peale greatly believed in the power of prayer. He said, "The flow of power between the creator and man is the world's greatest power. I know what prayer has done for me, and over and over again I have seen what it can do for others."[5]

Robert Schuller agrees. He states, "The greatest power in the world today is the power of people to communicate with Almighty God."[6]

Power Point

"**The greatest gift you can give anybody is to pray on their behalf.**"[8]
–George W. Bush

Noted authors Henry T. Blackaby and Claude V. King say that, after you pray, you need to do one more thing: "Immediately anticipate the activity of God in answer to your prayers. Expect Him to answer."[7]

Billy Graham believes that, when he prayed for his wife, power was released that brought healing into her body. Through prayer, you also have this force available to you. It is the power to overcome adversity and to change the course of natural events.

Power Point Question

How can you better activate the power of prayer?

_____

"[We] should always pray and not give up."
—Luke 18:1 (NIV)

Final Edition

News Headline

EXTRA! EXTRA!

Over One Million Cars Stolen

The National Insurance Institute reports that in America over one million cars are stolen each year. That is one car every twenty-three seconds.

When Alexander Berardi's car was stolen, he did not care about the other million or so vehicles that were stolen that year. For him, it was the day that the "bottom fell out."

As a young man, Alex went through a desperate season of his life. After his dad died, he floundered aimlessly. After graduating from high school and then he began working three jobs—one full-time and two part-time. Yet a recession was raging, and companies everywhere started laying off workers by the thousands. Alex became one of those statistics.

Two weeks after he lost his high-paying factory job, his apartment was burglarized. Because all his furniture was stolen, he was forced to sleep on the floor. Two months went by. His part-time jobs barely gave him enough money for food, and his cash was running out. His mother used her connections to get him a job working as an orderly at a local hospital. But the job was at night, and it, also, was only part-time.

His minimum-wage jobs did not provide enough money to cover his expenses. Soon, his landlord asked him to make other living arrangements. That was when he moved into his car. It was a ten-year-old forest green Ford Thunderbird, with three hubcaps, bald tires, and bad brakes—but it was home.

Things were bad, but early one morning a few weeks later, Alex would reach the lowest point of his young life.

He says, "I stood staring emotionless at the empty parking space where, only hours earlier, at the beginning of the night shift, I had left my car. Exhausted, I collapsed onto the curb. My world was ripping apart at the seams as I sat in the gutter, cold, hungry, retching, and writhing in pain from a sickening migraine headache. And now, I was homeless with nothing left but the clothes on my back."

TURNING FAILURE INTO SUCCESS

For the next several months, Alex lived on the streets. He did so while still trying to maintain a status-quo image at work because not too many employers want to keep a "bum" on their payroll. He discovered that he was far more resilient than he had realized and was capable of overcoming far more than he ever thought possible.

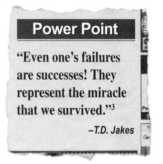

Power Point

"Even one's failures are successes! They represent the miracle that we survived."[3]

–T.D. Jakes

That understanding, plus the tenacity that he developed during those months, helped him to bounce back and become successful in business. Today, he speaks and motivates audiences around the world. His book, *Never Offer Your Comb to a Bald Man*, has sold over a million copies.

Alex says that if we live long enough, we will all experience our share of the good, the bad, and the ugly.[1] The object is not just to go through these experiences but to grow through them.[2]

Power Point Question

Do you create learning experiences out of hard times?

————————

"All things work together for good to them that love God,
[and]…
are called according to his purpose."
—Romans 8:28

News Headline

Final Edition

EXTRA! EXTRA!

Man Gives 30 Gallons Of Blood

According to the Red Cross, during his lifetime, an Oklahoma man has given over 30 gallons of blood.

In 1951, wanting to do something to help his fellow men, Bennie Willmann came up with the idea of donating his blood. Since blood can be donated only one pint at a time, he has made over 240 visits to the blood center.

Bennie says that he is just an ordinary man, a former Marine who fought during World War II. He exclaims, "Not being rich, I had to give what I could. What more could someone do than to help give life to another person?"

I salute Bernie for his compassion and commitment to helping others. He has the right priorities and is doing positive and inspiring things with his life.

To me, this is a good example of what a person's life should be based upon: reaching beyond one's own world to be a blessing to others.

What if more people, who were also financially successful, had the same value system and compassion as Bennie? In a lifetime, what kind of positive impact could their lives have on others?

As a reader of this book, you already have determined to achieve greater success. Why not achieve it based upon a life of giving and helping others? What greater purpose could you possess than to be a blessing to those in need?

Not only will your life have an impact on others, but you will be happier and more fulfilled. Psychologist William James stated, "The only truly happy people that I have ever known are those who have found a cause greater than themselves to live for."[1]

Having this perspective gives living a fresh meaning. It releases within you excitement and a new inner power that directs and propels your days.

In addition, you will be more blessed. Throughout the Bible, God brought increase to those who were willing to release what they had to help others. To be this kind of person, it will require you to personally redefine your meaning of success. For you, success must be measured, not only by what you get and/or accumulate but also by what you give.

Create your own "power points." Let them be the places and times where you have an opportunity to release blessings into other people's lives.

As Ted Turner says (who has given hundreds of millions of dollars to charities), "Regardless of how busy we get in our daily lives, we must take time out to identify areas and ways in which we can help others."[2]

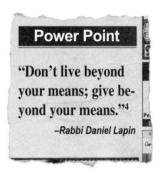

Power Point

"Don't live beyond your means; give beyond your means."[4]

–Rabbi Daniel Lapin

It might be giving clothes to charities or taking food to needy families. Maybe it is forming the habit of tipping at drive-thru windows and/or becoming a monthly donor to charities that are helping hurting people.

On the other hand, for you it could be setting a goal to give at least $100,000 per year to your church or synagogue. Maybe it is donating a million dollars to a cause that you deeply believe in.

Whatever you can do, begin now. As one of the greatest givers of all times, Bill Gates, says, "The dream is not about getting rich but about making a difference."[3]

Power Point Question

What actions can you take this week to positively impact others?

"A generous man devises generous things,
and by generosity he shall stand."
—Isaiah 32:8

Endnotes

Power Point #1: Massive Chrysler Shutdown
[1]TBN telethon; Tulsa Channel 17; 4/9/05.

Power Point #2: Wrong House Raided
[1]Rudolf Giuliana, *Leadership* (New York: Hyperion, 2002) 122.
[2]Donald Trump, *Trump: The Art of the Deal* (New York: Warner Books, 1987), 52.

Power Point #4: Nails Removed From Man's Head
[1]John Maxwell, *Attitude 101,* (Nashville: Thomas Nelson Publishers, 2003), 11.
[2]Ibid, 12.
[3]Ibid, 5.

Power Point #5: Giuliani Starts Investment Firm
[1]Rudolf Giuliani, *Leadership* (New York: Hyperion, 2002), 117.
[2]Idid., 43.
[3]Ibid., xi – xii.
[4]Ibid., xii.

Power Point #6: Last Pontiac Rolls Off Line
[1]*Life is a Collection of Seasons*, General Norman Schwarzkopf, USA Retired
[2]Henry David Thoreau

Power Point #7: Teen Surfs After Shark Attack
[1]"Girl Who Lost Arm to Shark Surfs in Meet," *The Associated Press*, posted on Herald.com, 11 January 2004. <http://www.miami.com/mld/miamiherald/sports/7682153.htm> (14 January 20, 2004).
[2]Jill Lieber, "Teen Riding Wave of Amazing Grace," *USA Today*, 19 March 2004, 15C.
[3]Ibid.
[4]<http://topicsites.com/booker-t-washington.booker-t-washington-quotes.htm>

Power Point #8: Zig Ziglar Receives Award

[1]*Get Motivated Workbook* (Tampa, Florida: Peter Lowe Seminars, 2003), 18, and <http://ziglartraining.com/Ziglar/zigziglar.do> (22 January 2004)

[2]<www.quotationspage.com/search.php3?Author=Zig+Ziglar&file=other> (November 17, 2004)

Power Point #9: Government's Eye Never Sleeps

[1]T.D. Jakes, *Loose That Man and Let Him Go* (Tulsa: Albury Press, 1995), 93.

[2]Laurie Beth Jones, *Jesus-Led* (New York: Hyperion, 1996), 22.

[3]Author's quote archives; source unknown.

[4]Richard Exley, *The Rhythm of Life* (Tulsa: Honor Books, 1987), 60.

[5]Donald Trump, *Trump: Surviving at the Top* (New York: Farrar, Straus and Cudahy, 1956), 724.

[6]T.D. Jakes, *Reposition Yourself* (New York: Atria Books, 2007),215

Power Point #10: Charity Gets Moving in New Van

[1]Anthony Robbins, *Unlimited Power*, pg 278.

2 Tom Hopkins, *How to Master the Art of Selling* (Scottsdale, AZ: Tom Hopkins Intn'l, 1982), 93.

Power Point #11: Survival Attitude Helps Downed Pilot

[1]Bruce, B. Auster, "One Amazing Kid," *U.S. News and World Report*, June 19, 1995. <http://www.f-16.net/library/stories/ogrady.html> (January 12, 2004).

[2]Dexter Yager, speech, Gooch Free Enterprise Weekend, Knoxville, Tennessee, September 1990.

Power Point #13: Resort Town Bans Ties

[1]Johnny Carson, <http://www.brainyquote.com/quotes/quotes/j/johnnycars158444.html>

[2]Joe Gibbs, *Game Plans For Success* (Boston: Little, Brown, and Company, 1995), 155.

[3]Zig Ziglar, July 1990 Success Seminar, Honolulu, Hawaii.

[4]Joe Griffith, *Speaker's Library of Business Stories* (Englewood Cliffs, N.J.: Prentice Hall, 1990), 266-67.

[5]Ibid.

Power Point #14: Collision with Pole Restores Eyesight

[1]Jerome Edmondson, *Maximizing Misfortune* (Shippensburg, Pennsylvania: Treasure House, 2003), 53.

[2]Ibid., 56.

Power Point #15: Swimmer Told Not to Spit in Pool

[1]Van Crouch, *Winning 101: Insight and Motivation to Help You Achieve Excellence* (Tulsa: Honor Books, 1995), 108

[2]Personal conversation, St. Louis, Missouri, October 1999.

Power Point #16: Man Searches for Absentee Dad

[1]Dr. James Dobson, *Straight Talk* (Dallas: World Publishing, 1991), 62.

[2]Lee Iacocca, *Talking Straight*, (New York: Bantam Books, 1988), 24.

[3]*God's Little Devotional Book for Dads* (Tulsa: Honor Books, 1995), 219.

[4]Dads Get Creative, *USA Today*, June 16, 2010, pg 2D.

[5]Lee Iacocca, *Talking Straight*, 23.

Power Point #17: Doctors Warned About Exploding Patients

[1]Tim LaHaye, *Anger is a Choice* (Grand Rapids: Zondervan, 1982), 156.

[2]T.D. Jakes, *Reposition Yourself* (New York: Atria Books; 2007),148.

[3]Derek Prince, *God's Remedy for Rejection* (New Kensington, PA: Whitaker House, 1993), 70-71.

[4]LaHaye, *Anger is a Choice*, 156.

Power Point #18: Turtle Falls from Sky, Hits Man Driving Convertible, Causes Crash, Sends Him to Hospital

[1]Denis Waitley, *Timing is Everything,* (Nashville: Thomas Nelson Publishers, 1992), 6-7.

[2]Ruth Stafford Peale

Power Point #19: Swimmer Loses Trunks During Race

[1]Paul G. Stoltz, *Adversity Quotient: Turning Obstacles into Opportunities* (New York: John Wiley & Sons, 1997), 67.

[2]Anthony Robbins, *Unlimited Power* (New York: Fawcett Columbine, 1987), 198.

[3]<http://www.usatennisflorida.usta.com/news/fullstory.sps?iNewsID=51348&i type=1107&iCategoryID=>

Power Point #20: Fish Removed From Man's Nose

[1]Les Brown, *Live Your Dreams* (New York: William Morrow and Company, 1992), 41.

[2]Ibid., 49.

Power Point #21: Cadillac Crashes into Bedroom

[1]Lewis Lord, *U.S. News and World Report*, 6 December 1999, 76.

[2]<http://www.pbs.org/wgbh/amex/quizshow/sfeature/part5.html>

[3]Dr. Joyce Brothers, *The Successful Woman* (New York: Simon and Schuster, 1988), 49.

[4]Ibid.

[5]Alvin Toffler from Powershift: *Knowledge, Wealth, and Violence at the Edge of the 21st Century*, 2, 1990, quoted in Leonard Roy Frank, ed., Random House *Webster's Quotionary* (New York: Random House, 2001), 430.

[6]Harvey McKay, *Beware the Naked Man Who Offers You His Shirt* (New York: Ivy Books, 1990), 78.

Power Point #22: Governor Schwarzenegger Announces Recovery Plan

[1]<http://www.uk-learning.net/t20288.html>

[2]Leo Rosten, *Leo Rosten's Treasury of Jewish Quotations* (New York: McGraw-Hill Book Company/The Jewish Publication Society of America, 1972), 182.

Power Point #23: Blind Man Robs Bank, Then Cannot Find Way Out

[1]Leo Rosten, *Leo Rosten's Treasury of Jewish Quotations* (New York: McGraw-Hill Book Company/The Jewish Publication Society of America, 1972), 233.

Power Point #24: Stocks Ignoring Bad Economic News

[1]Leo Tice, *Smart Talk for Achieving Your Potential* (Seattle, Washington: Pacific Institute Publishing, 1995), 59.

[2]Ibid., 62.

Power Point #25: Joe Gibbs Rejoins NASCAR

[1]Ray Didinger, *Game Plans* (Boston: Little, Brown, and Company, 1995), 39.

Power Point #26: 92-year-old Woman gets 30-year Mortgage

[1]John Mason, *An Enemy Called Average* (Tulsa: Harrison House, 1990). 52.

Power Point #27: Man Hit by Lightning on Golf Course

[1]Personal conversation with author, Indianapolis, Indiana, October 1997.

[2]Zig Ziglar, *Top Performance* (New York: Berkley Books, 1987), 43.

[3]TV Special, Tulsa Community College, Channel 21, Tulsa, Oklahoma, 15 March 2002

[4]*A Better Way to Live* (New York, Batam Books, 1990), 95

[5]Norman Vincent Peale, *Bible Power for Successful Living* (New York: Peale Center for Christian Living, 1993), 130.

Power Point #28: Man Come Out of Coma

[1]Personal conversation with author.

Power Point #29: Toilet Paper Theft Causes Firing

[1]J.C. Watts, *Decision* Magazine, July 2004, 15.

Power Point #30: Car Falls Seven Floors

[1]Robert Schuller, *Power Thoughts* (New York: Harper-Collins Publishers, 1993), 21.

[2]<http://www.crystalcathedral.org/about/aboutrhs.html> (20 January 2004).

[3]Robert Schuller, *Power Thoughts* (New York: Harper-Collins Publishers, 1993), 92.

[4]Ibid.

[5]Robert Schuller, *Power Thoughts* (1993), 67.

Power Point #31: Couple Marries at Airport

[1]Dick Cheney, *USA Today*, June 9, 2006, pg 15.

Power Point #32: Government Cares for Monkeys

[1]For a discussion of this topic, please refer to Kenneth Blanchard, William Oncken, Jr., and Hal Burrows, *The One-Minute Manager Meets the Monkey* (New York: Quill William Morrow, 1989).

[2]Ibid.

Power Point #34: Quarterback Leaves Pro Bowl Early

[1]Anthony Robbins, *Unlimited Power* (New York: Fawcett Columbine, 1986), 298.

Power Point #35: With Low-Cal Movement, Less is More

[1]Laurie Beth Jones, *Jesus-CEO* (New York: Hyperion Press, 1955), 77.

Power Point #36: Palm Desert Buys University

[1]<http://www.thinkarete.com/quotes/by_teacher/abraham_lincoln> (August 16, 2004)

Power Point #37: Bugging Devices Cause Political Furor

[1]*Business Travel News*, June 1995.

[2]Charles R. Smith, "Big Brother on Board," *newsmax.com*, 11 December 2003. <http://www.newsmax.com/archives/articles/2003/12/10/213653.shtml> (August 13, 2004)

[3]Ibid.

[4]Meeting News, 8 April 2004, 1.

Power Point #38: Parents Made Kids Eat Rats and Roaches

[1]Robert H. Schuller, *Self-Esteem: The New Reformation* (Waco: Word Books, 1982), 34.

[2]Zig Ziglar, *Top Performance* (New York: Berkley Books, 1986), 91.

[3]Colin Powell, personal conversation with author, Indianapolis, 1997.

Power Point #39: New Lease on Life

[1]Edna Harrison-Harlin, *A Second Chance at Love* (Garden Grove, CA: New Lease Publishers, 1984), 60.

Power Point #40: Man Hugs Tree to Escape Fine

[1]Dewey Freidel, *Real Men Wear Boxer Shorts* (Shippenburg, Pennsylvania: Destiny Image Publishers, 1995), 139.

[2]<http://www.cellularmemory.net/PEC.htm>

[3]Dewey Freidel, *Real Men*, 139.

[4]USA Today, 11 January 2001, 1D.

[5]Jack Canfield and Mark Victor Hansen, *Dare to Win* (Newport Beach, California: self-published, 1988), 90.

Power Point #42: Survivors Gather at Reunion

[1]*USA Today*, January 19, 2009, pg 3A.

Power Point #43: Giant Sinkhole Swallows Home

[1]Gary Smalley, *Hidden Key of a Loving, Lasting Marriage,* (Grand Rapids, MI.: Zondervan Publishing House, 1988), 18-19.

[2]Ibid, 332.

[3]Ibid, 18-19.

Power Point #44: Biggest Loser Gains

[1]Jim Collins, *Good to be Great* (Jim Collins, New York: Harper Business, 2001), 13.

[2]Gary Richardson

Power Point #46: Cruise Ship Runs Aground

[1]Gavin and Patti MacLeod, *Back on Course* (Old Tappen, New Jersey: Flemming H. Revell Company, 1987), 93.

[2]Ibid., 140.

Power Point #47: City Starts Automated Trash Removal

[1]Joe Griffith, *Speaker's Library of Business Stories* (Englewood Cliffs, New Jersey: Prentice Hall, 1990), 356.

[2]Ronnie Belanger and Brian Mast, eds., *Profiles of Success* (North Brunswick, New Jersey: Bridge-Logos Publishing, 1999), 160.

[3]Ibid., 59.

[4]Author's quote archives; source unknown.

Power Point #48: Graham Awarded Congressional Medal

[1]"Billy Graham," *Tulsa World*, 9 May 1996, A16 (Editorial).

[2]Vernon McLellan, *Billy Graham: A Tribute from Friends* (Colorado Springs, Colorado: Warner Books, 2002), 25.

[3]Billy Graham, *Just As I Am* (Carmel, New York: Guideposts [by special arrangement with Harper San Francisco Publishers], 1997), 128.

[4]Ibid.

[5]Edwin Louis Cole, *Courage: A Book for Champions* (Tulsa: Honor Books, 1985), 90.

[6]John Wooden, *They Call Me Coach* (Waco, Texas: Work Books, 1985).

[7]<http://www.brainyquote.com/quotes/authors/b/billy_graham.html> (10 May 2004)

Power Point #49: Asian Elephant Born in Captivity

[1]Myles Munroe, *The Principles and Power of Vision* (New Kensington: Whitaker House, 2003), 99.

[2]Ibid., 217.

[3]Ibid., 103.

[4]Lee Iacocca, *Iacocca—An Autobiography* (New York: Bantam Books, 1984), 281.

[5]Bill Gates, "Technology," *Price-Costco Connection*, December 1996, 43.

Power Point #50: Woman Rides Out Tornado in Bathtub

[1]Tom Landry, *An Autobiography—Tom Landry* (New York: Harper Paperbacks, 1990), 286.

Power Point #51: Airline Sends Kids to Wrong Cities

[1]Stephen Covey, *The Seven Habits of Highly Effective People,* (New York: Simon and Schuster, 1989) 99.

[2]Earl Nightingale

Power Point #52: Cities Finding Gold in Parking Fees and Fines

[1]*Travel Weekly*, June 1995, 12.

Power Point #53: Governor Say's "Thanks" to Firms

[1]Joe Griffith, *Speaker's Library of Business Stories* (Englewood Cliffs, New Jersey: Prentice Hall, 1990), 266.

[2]Zig Ziglar, *Top Performance* (New York: Berkley Books, 1986), 178.

[3]Richard Capen, Jr., *Finish Strong* (San Francisco: Harper/Zondervan, 1996), 81.

[4]*The Power Newsletter* (Amway), March 1996, 7.

[5]Wanda Loskot, *SanMarketing.com* <http://www.sanemarketing.com/articles/tank.html> (November 5, 2004)

Power Point #57: Can Found Inside of Fish

[1]Les Brown, *Live your Dream* (New York: William Morrow and Company, 1992), 211.

Power Point #59: Student Jailed for Udder Nonsense

[1]Anthony Robbins, *Unlimited Power* (New York: Fawcett Columbine, 1986), 220.

Power Point #61: Vegetarians Becoming Flexitarians

[1]<http://en.proverbia.net/citasautor.asp?nombre=George+Bernard&apellidos=Shaw&autor=16652&page=9> (December 2, 2004)

[2]<http://www.zaadz.com/quotes/authors/john_h_patterson/> (August 9, 2004)

[3]Jacquelyn Wonder and Priscilla Donovan, *The Flexibility Factor* (Ballantine Books, 1991), 6.

Power Point #62: Doorman Refuses to Hail Cab

[1]<http://www.cnn.com/HEALTH/library/EP/00002.html> (October 27, 2004)

[2]"It's Never Too Late to Start Living a Healthier Lifestyle," Prime Life Styles. <http://www.goerie.com/primelifestyles/it_s_never_too_late_to_start_l.html> (August 9,2004)

[3]Kenneth W. Cooper, *Aerobics* (New York: Bantam Books, 1968), 24.

[4]Ibid., inside cover of book jacket.

[5]<http://www.cnn.com/HEALTH/library/EP/00002.html> (October 27, 2004)

Power Point #63: Woman Living in Man's Closet

NEED CITING INFORMATION ON:

[1]Robert Nelson, quoted in *Skills for Success* (Bristol, Vermont: The Soundview Executive Book Summaries, 1989) 90.

[2]John Maxwell, *Developing the Leader Within You* (Nashville: Nelson Books, 1993), 28.

[3]David Ingles, personal conversation with author, June 1999.

[4]*Skills for Success*, 89.

[5]Joyce Meyer, meeting at Mabee Center, Tulsa, Oklahoma, June 2003.

Power Point #64: Dead Woman Gets Job Back

[1]Arvella Schuller, *The Positive Family* (Garden City, NJ: Doubleday-Galilee, 1982), 31.

[2]Jan Stoop and Betty Southward, *The Grandmother Book* (Nashville: Thomas Nelson Publishers, 1993), 135.

[3]Ibid., 38.

Power Point #65: Saboteurs Derail Train

[1]Stephen Covey, *First Things First* (New York: Simon and Schuster, 1994), 36.

[2]Stephen Covey, *The Seven Habits of Highly Effective People* (New York: Simon and Schuster, 1989), 148.

Power Points for Increase

Power Point #67: Globe Littered with Land Mines

[1]John R. Noe, *Peak Performance Priciples for High Achievers* (New York: Frederick Fell Publishers, 1984), 96.

[2]Ibid., 41.

[3]Ibid., 96.

[4]The first three "Land Mines of the Past" quotes come from Gemmy Allen, "Supervision," online course, Mountain View College, Dallas, Texas, 1998. Source: <http://ollie.dcccd.edu/mgmt1374/book_contents/2planning/plng_process/change.htm> (August 24, 2004)

[5]*National Inquirer*, 20 June 2000, 20.

[6]Ibid.

[7]Ibid.

[8]John R. Noe, *Peak Performance*, 105.

Power Point #68: Contest Officials Search for God

[1]Stephen R. Covey, *The Seven Habits of Highly Effective People* (New York: Simon and Schuster, 1989), 277.

[2]Ibid., 284.

[3]Florence Littauer, *Dare to Dream* (Waco, Texas: W Publishing Group, 1991), 12.

Power Point #69: Varmints Stink Up School

[1]Phillip C. McGraw, *Life Strategies* (New York: Hyperion, 1999), 68.

[2]Phillip C. McGraw, *Self Matters* (New York: Simon and Schuster, 2001), 192.

[3]General Norman Schwarzkopf, personal conversation, St. Louis, Missouri.

[4]John Mason, Hawaii Increase Event, March 1995.

[5]Mark Victor Hansen, IBI Seminar, Long Beach, California, November 1994.

[6]Dexter Yager, *Don't Let Anybody Steal Your Dreams* (Charlotte, NC: Internet Services, 1993), 31.

[7]Charles Swindoll, *Living Above the Level of Mediocrity* (Waco, Texas: Word Books, 1987), 81.

[8]Colin Powell, personal conversation with author, Indiana, October 1997.

[9]*Ministries Today*, March 1999, 24.

Power Point #70: Chick-fil-a Wins Quality Award

[1]<http://www.chick-fil-a.com>

[2]See also S. Truett Cathy, *It Is Easier to Succeed Than to Fail* (Nashville: Thomas Nelson Publishers, 1989), 16.

[3]Robert Schuller, *Power Thoughts* (New York: Harper-Collins, 1993), 65.

[4]Ibid., 37.

[5]Myles Munroe, *The Principles and Power of Vision* (New Kensington: Whitaker House, 2003), 198.

[6]Schuller, *Power Thoughts*, 142.

[7]S. Truett Cathy, *It is Easier to Succeed*, 13.

Power Point #71: $2 Million Paid for Lunch

[1]<www.nyse.com/press/1022834145706.html> (27 August 2004)

[2]<www.pbs.org/wgbh/pages/frontline/shows/scandal/inside/cron.html> (27 August 2004)

Power Point #72: Many Still in the Dark

[1]Tulsa World, 17 June 2004, A-12.

[2]James Stovall, *You Don't Have to be Blind to See* (Nashville: Thomas Nelson Publishers, 1996), 2.

[3]Myles Munroe, *The Principles and Power of Vision* (New Kensington: Whitaker House, 2003), 11.

[4]Ibid., 11-12.

[5]Ibid., 13.

[6]Ibid., 32.

Power Point #73: Elevator Suddenly Plunges

[1]Tom Peters, *Thriving on Chaos* (New York: Harper-Perennial, 1987), 108.

Power Point #74: Star is Rich and Lonely

[1]Dr. Patrick Quillen, Healing Secrets from the Bible (Canton, OH.: The Leader Company, 1995), 21.

[2]Catherine Marshall, To Live Again (New York: Fawcett World Library, 1970) 42.

[3] Ibid, 45.

[4] Ibid, 42.

Power Point #75: Star has Deathbed Regrets

[1] Stephen R. Covey, *The Seven Habits of Highly Effective People* (New York: Simon and Schuster, 1989), 97.

Power Point #76: Student Honestly Linked to Discounts

[1] Joe Griffith, *Speaker's Library of Business Stories* (Englewood Cliffs, New Jersey: Prentice Hall, 1990), 152.

[2] Ibid.

Power Point #77: Sheriff is Resident of Jail He Built

[1] Lou Tice, *Smart Talk* (Seattle, Washington: Pacific Institute Publishing, 1995), 11.

[2] Suze Orman, *9 Steps to Financial Freedom* (New Yor: Crown Publishers, 1997), 7.

Power Point #78: Bush Parachutes for his 80th Birthday

[1] Zig Ziglar, *Courtship After Marriage* (Nashville: Thomas Nelson Publishers, 1990), 240.

[2] Billy Graham during guest appearance on Larry King Live, date unknown.

[3] Zig Ziglar, *Courtship After Marriage*, 19.

[4] *Tulsa World*, 8 September 2004, C-6.

[5] Gary Smalley, *Hidden Keys of a Loving, Lasting Marriage* (Grand Rapids, Michigan: Zondervan Publishing House, 1988), 42.

[6] Arvella Schuller, *The Positive Family* (Garden City, NJ: Doubleday-Galilee, 1982), 67.

[7] Randy J. Gibbs, *20/20 Vision* (New York: Daybreak Books, 1998), 96.

Power Point #79: Arab Sheik Buys 40 College Degrees

[1] Les Brown, *Live Your Dreams* (New York: William Morrow and Company, 1992), 49.

Power Point #80: Jet Crashes Short of Runway

[1]Julie Schmit, *USA Today*, 4 April 1995, B1.

[2]Herbert Freudenberger, *Burn Out* (Garden City, New York: Anchor Press, 1980), 210.

Power Point #81: Wife Victimized by Chiseling Romeo

[1]Jim Guinn, "Christian Con Men: The New Breed," *RMAI*, Fall/Winter 1995.

[2]Myles Munroe, Global Leadership Summit, Nassau, Bahamas, 12 November 2002.

[3]Marilyn Hickey, ICBM Conference, Tulsa, Oklahoma, 1 June 2002.

[4]Ken Blanchard, *The Heart of a Leader* (Tulsa: Honor Books, 1999), 56.

Power Point #82: Bird Causes Power Outage at Airport

[1]<http://www.tulsaworld.com/archivesearch/Search/ArchiveArticleConfirm.asp?articleID=362889>

[2]Jack Canfield, Mark Victor Hansen, and Les Hewitt, *The Power of Focus* (Deerfield Beach, FL: Health Communications, 2000), 173.

[3]Gary Smalley, *Hidden Keys of a Loving, Lasting Marriage* (Grand Rapids, Michigan: Zondervan Publishing House, 1988), 267.

[4]Dennis Byrd, *Rise and Walk: The Trials and Triumph of Dennis Byrd* (New York: HarperCollins, 1993).

[5]Phillip C. McGraw, *Life Strategies* (New York: Hyperion, 1999), 167.

[6]Phillip C. McGraw, *Life Strategies*, 167.

Power Point #83: Man Trapped in Outhouse Overnight

[1]Dr. Patrick Quillin, "Biblical Health Secrets," Bob Harrison Hawaii Increase Event, March 1999.

[2]Edwin Feldman, *How to Use Your Time,* 8.

[3]Edwin Feldman, *How to Use Your Time to Get Things Done,* (New York: Fredrick Fell Publishers, 1968), 62.

[4]George Shinn, *Miracle of Motivation*, (Wheaton: Living Books, 1981), 168.

[5]Ibid.

Power Point #85: Fuss Over Backward Cap

[1]Tim Redmond, *Words of Promise*, (Tulsa: Honor Books, 1995), 94.

[1]Harvey McKay, *Beware the Naked Man Who Offers You His Shirt*, (New York: Ivy Books, 1990), 373.

Power Point #86: Healthy Habits Reduce Heart Disease

[1]Linda Ciampa, "Healthy Habits Can Reduce Risk of Heart Disease," CNN, 9 November 1999. <http://www.cnn.com/HEALTH/9911/09/heart.food/> (21 January 2004)

[2]Dr. Chris Enriquez, M.D., *The Healthy Life* (New Kensington: Whitaker House, 2004), 16.

[3]Dr. Patrick Quillin, *Healing Secrets from the Bible* (Canton, Ohio: The Leader Company, 1995), 1.

[4]Ibid., 7.

[5]Ibid., 13.

Power Point #88: Newsboys Band Takes Arena with Them

[1]Newsboys, *Shine* (New Kensington, Pennsylvania: Whitaker House, 2002), 42.

[2]Frank Bettger, *How I Raised Myself from Failure to Success in Selling* (New York: Simon & Schuster, 1982), 156.

[3]Anne M. Obarski, *Surprising Secrets of Mystery Shoppers: 10 Steps to Quality Service That Keep Customers Coming Back!* (Tarentum, Pennsylvania: Word Association Publishers), 77.

[4]Ibid., 18-19.

[5]Tom Peters, *Thriving on Chaos* (New York: Harper-Perennial, 1987), 108.

Power Point #89: Long Ride to Harvard

[1]Khadijah Williams <www.everydaycitizen.com>

Power Point #90: Hotel Faces Lawsuits on Surcharges

[1]<http://espn.go.com/nfl/new/2003/0430/1547404.html>

[2]Deepak Chopra, *The Seven Spiritual Laws of Success* (San Rafael, California: Amber-Allen Publishing, 1994), 89.

Power Point #91: Man Forgets Wife at Gas Station

[1]Charles Stanley, *The Wonderful Spirit-Filled Life* (Nashville: Thomas Nelson Publishers, 1995), 77.

Power Point #92: Robber Steals Money From Salvation Army Kettle

[1]Don Ostrom, *Millionaire in the Pew* (Tulsa: Insight Publishing group, 2004), 112.

[2]Ibid., 90.

[3]Rabbi Daniel Lapin, *Thou Shall Prosper* (Hoboken, New York: John Wiley and Sons, 2002), 307.

Power Point #93: Thieves Steal Family History

[1]Rudolph Giuliani, *Leadership* (New York: Hyperion, 2002), 62.

[2]Ibid., 64.

Power Point #94: Mother Battles Gator to Save Son

[1]Dr. Robert Anthony, *How to Make the Impossible Possible* (New York: Berkley Books, 1996), 66.

[2]Cherie Carter-Scott, television interview, 28 May 2003.

[3]<http://www.quotationspage.com/quotes/Henry_Ford> (December 23, 2004)

[4]Bill Bright, *Believing God for the Impossible* (San Bernardino, California: Here's Life Publishers, 1979), 42, 46.

[5]Anthony Robbins, *Unlimited Power* (New York: Fawcett Columbine, 1986), 15.

[6]Cherie Carter-Scott, television interview, 28 May 2003.

Power Point #95: dead Woman Sheds a Tear

[1]http://www.brainyquote.com/quotes/authors/r/robert_collier.html(December 22, 2004)

Power Point #96: Cancer Claims Ted Kennedy

[1]Rick Warren, http://www.southasianconnection.com/blogs/18/Interview-with-Rick-Warren-by-Paul-Bradshaw.html

Power Point #97: New Movie Features 10-Minute Segments

[1]Joe Griffith, *Speaker's Library of Business Stories* (Englewood Cliffs, N.J.: Prentice Hall, 1990), 355.

Power Point #98: Chef Fired for Good Cooking

[1]Tom Peters, *Thriving on Chaos* (New York: Harper-Perennial, 1987), 102.

Power Point #99: Prayer Makes a Difference

[1]Dana Sterling, "Praying to Get Well," *Tulsa World*, 19 December 1996, A1-2.

[2]Ibid.

[3]Ibid.

[4]Charles Stanley, *The Wonderful Spirit-filled Life* (Nashville: Thomas Nelson Publishers, 1992), 5.

[5]Norman Vincent Peale, *The Power of the Plus Factor* (Old Tappan, New Jersey: Fleming H Revell, 1987), 122

[6]Robert Schuller, *Positive Prayers for Power-filled Living* (New York: Hawthorne Books, 1976), inside the flap of book jacket.

[7]Henry T. Blackaby and Claude V. King, *Experiencing God* (Nashville: Broadman & Hollman, 1998), 180-81.

[8]Barbara Wheeler, M.D., "America's Prayer Network Newsletter," Washington, D.C., September 2004.

Power Point #100: Over One Million Cars Stolen

[1]Alexander J. Berardi, *Never Offer Your Comb to a Bald Man* (Novato, California: New World Library, 2001), 94.

[2]Ibid.,

[3]T.D. Jakes, *Loose That Man and Let Him Go* (Tulsa: Albury Press, 1995), 95.

Power Point #101: Man Gives 30 Gallons of Blood

[1]Richard Exley, *The Rhythm of Life* (Tulsa: Honor Books, 1987), 108.

[2]James Stovel, *Success Secrets of Super Achievers* (Tulsa: Narrative Television Network, 2001), 153.

[3]Bill Gates, "Technology," *Price-Costco Connection*, December 1996, 43.

[4]Rabbi Daniel Lapin, *Thou Shalt Prosper* (Hoboken, New Jersey: John Wiley and Sons, 2002), 298.